WHAT IF IT HAPPENED TO YOU:
VIOLENT CRIMES AND VICTIMS' RIGHTS

by
Margaret C. Jasper

Oceana's Legal Almanac Series:
Law for the Layperson

2003
Oceana Publications, Inc.
Dobbs Ferry, New York

Information contained in this work has been obtained by Oceana Publications from sources believed to be reliable. However, neither the Publisher nor its authors guarantee the accuracy or completeness of any information published herein, and neither Oceana nor its authors shall be responsible for any errors, omissions or damages arising from the use of this information. This work is published with the understanding that Oceana and its authors are supplying information, but are not attempting to render legal or other professional services. If such services are required, the assistance of an appropriate professional should be sought.

You may order this or any Oceana publication by visiting Oceana's website at http://www.oceanalaw.com

Library of Congress Control Number: 2003113180

ISBN: 0-379-11380-5

Oceana's Legal Almanac Series: Law for the Layperson
ISSN 1075-7376

©2003 by Oceana Publications, Inc.

Manufactured in the United States of America on acid-free paper.

To My Husband Chris

Your love and support
are my motivation and inspiration

-and-

In memory of my son, Jimmy

Table of Contents

CHAPTER 1:
PROFILE OF VIOLENCE IN AMERICA

CHAPTER 2:
PUNISHMENT

CHAPTER 3:
VIOLENCE AGAINST CHILDREN

CHAPTER 4:
VIOLENCE AGAINST THE ELDERLY

CHAPTER 5:
VIOLENCE AGAINST WOMEN

CHAPTER 6:
STALKING

CHAPTER 7:
SCHOOL VIOLENCE

APPENDICES

ABOUT THE AUTHOR

MARGARET C. JASPER is an attorney engaged in the general practice of law in South Salem, New York, concentrating in the areas of personal injury and entertainment law. Ms. Jasper holds a Juris Doctor degree from Pace University School of Law, White Plains, New York, is a member of the New York and Connecticut bars, and is certified to practice before the United States District Courts for the Southern and Eastern Districts of New York, the United States Court of Appeals for the Second Circuit, and the United States Supreme Court.

Ms. Jasper has been appointed to the panel of arbitrators of the American Arbitration Association and the law guardian panel for the Family Court of the State of New York, is a member of the Association of Trial Lawyers of America, and is a New York State licensed real estate broker and member of the Westchester County Board of Realtors, operating as Jasper Real Estate, in South Salem, New York. She maintains a website at http://www.JasperLawOffice.com.

Ms. Jasper is the author and general editor of the following legal almanacs: AIDS Law; The Americans with Disabilities Act; Animal Rights Law; The Law of Attachment and Garnishment; Bankruptcy Law for the Individual Debtor; Individual Bankruptcy and Restructuring; Banks and their Customers; The Law of Buying and Selling; The Law of Capital Punishment; The Law of Child Custody; Commercial Law; Consumer Rights Law; The Law of Contracts; Copyright Law; Credit Cards and the Law; The Law of Debt Collection; Dictionary of Selected Legal Terms; The Law of Dispute Resolution; The Law of Drunk Driving; Education Law; Elder Law; Employee Rights in the Workplace; Employment Discrimination Under Title VII; Environmental Law; Estate Planning; Everyday Legal Forms; Executors and Personal Representatives: Rights and Responsibilities; Harassment in the Workplace; Health Care and Your Rights. Home Mortgage Law Primer; Hospital Liability Law; Identity Theft and How To Protect Yourself; Insurance

Law; The Law of Immigration; International Adoption; Juvenile Justice and Children's Law; Labor Law; Landlord-Tenant Law; The Law of Libel and Slander; Living Together: Practical Legal Issues; Marriage and Divorce; The Law of Medical Malpractice; Motor Vehicle Law; The Law of No-Fault Insurance; Nursing Home Negligence; The Law of Obscenity and Pornography; Patent Law; The Law of Personal Injury; Privacy and the Internet: Your Rights and Expectations Under the Law; Probate Law; The Law of Product Liability; Real Estate Law for the Homeowner and Broker; Religion and the Law; The Right to Die; Law for the Small Business Owner; Social Security Law; Special Education Law; The Law of Speech and the First Amendment; Teenagers and Substance Abuse; Trademark Law; Victim's Rights Law; The Law of Violence Against Women; Welfare: Your Rights and the Law; What if it Happened to You: Violent Crimes and Victims' Rights; What if it Happened to You: Violent Crimes and Victims' Rights; What if the Product Doesn't Work: Warranties & Guarantees; Workers' Compensation Law; and Your Child's Legal Rights: An Overview.

INTRODUCTION

America is a violent society. All one needs to do is turn on the evening news to validate that statement. Stories of murder, rape, and other violent acts are presented in all of their gory details, and are no longer sensational because they have become all too common. It appears that people have become desensitized to the violence—it is just too much to handle.

Violence in America far surpasses any other industrialized nation. As discussed in this almanac, the statistics on violence in America are alarming. In fact, some foreign embassies have issued safety warnings to their citizens planning to visit America.

This almanac presents an overview of the many situations involving violent behavior that an individual may confront, including domestic violence, school violence, and violence in the workplace. Violence targeted at specific groups is also discussed, including violence against children, women, the elderly, and minority groups.

This almanac also explores the underlying causes that are attributable to violent behavior, and the characteristics common to the victims and perpetrators of violence. The criminal justice system's attempt to punish violent behavior is also discussed, as well as the procedures a crime victim will likely encounter within the system.

Further, the mechanisms set up to compensate the victims of violent crime and the resources available to crime victims in dealing with the after-effects of victimization are also set forth in this almanac.

The Appendix provides resource directories, applicable statutes, and other pertinent information and data. The Glossary contains definitions of many of the terms used throughout the almanac.

CHAPTER 1:
PROFILE OF VIOLENCE IN AMERICA

THE NATIONAL CRIME VICTIMIZATION SURVEY

The National Crime Victimization Survey (NCVS) is America's primary source of information on criminal victimization. Data is obtained from a nationally representative sample of approximately 43,000 households, comprising nearly 80,000 persons aged 12 or older. The household members surveyed are asked about the frequency, characteristics, and consequences of victimization.

The NCVS survey enables the U.S. Department of Justice, Bureau of Justice Statistics (BJS) to estimate the rate of victimization for a variety of violent offenses, and describes the vulnerability to crime by the population as a whole, as well as by segments of the population such as women, the elderly, youth, and members of racial and ethnic groups. The most recent NCVS survey, which covers the time period from 1993 through 2001, forms the basis for the statistics set forth in this chapter.

CLASSIFICATION OF WEAPONS

According to the NCVS survey, weapons were classified as follows:

Firearms

Firearms include handguns, such as pistols, revolvers, and derringers; shotguns; rifles; and other firearms. BB guns, pellet guns and air rifles are excluded from this category.

Sharp Objects

Sharp objects include knives and other sharp edged and/or pointed objects, such as scissors, ice picks, and axes.

Blunt Objects

Blunt objects include rocks, clubs, blackjacks, bats, and metal pipes.

Other Weapons

Other weapons include ropes, chains, poison, martial arts weapons, BB guns, and other objects that could not be classified.

TRENDS IN VIOLENT CRIME

According to the NCVS survey, violent crime actually declined 54% from 1993 through 2001, and weapon violence decreased 59%. In addition, the rate of firearm violence fell 63%.

During this same time period, the number of murders declined 36% while the number of murders by firearms dropped 41%. In 1993, 72% of homicides of persons age 12 or older were committed with firearms. In 2001, 66% of such homicides were committed with firearms.

According to the NCVS survey, the rates of firearm violence for blacks and Hispanics fell relatively more than the rate for whites. In 1993 blacks and Hispanics were victims of firearm violence at a rate of 13 firearm crimes per 1,000 persons, about 3 times the rate for whites. By 2001 the rate for blacks had fallen to about 4 per 1,000, roughly 2.5 times that for whites. In 2001 Hispanics experienced firearm violence at a rate per 1,000 similar to those for both blacks and whites.

In addition, from 1993 to 2001, rates of violence involving firearms declined among all age groups. The decline was greatest among the youngest victims. By 2001, persons age 12-14 had experienced a 97% decrease in the rate of firearm violence, and those age 15-17 had a 77% decline.

WEAPON VIOLENCE

Estimates from the NCVS survey indicate that an annual average of approximately 2.3 million (26%) of the estimated 8.9 million violent crimes in the United States were committed by offenders armed with guns, knives, or other objects used as weapons, as follows:

Firearms

According to the NCVS survey, an annual average rate of 4 crimes per 1,000 persons aged 12 or older were committed by offenders using firearms. The average annual violent victimizations by firearm totalled approximately 847,000 and, about 7 out of 8 of these crimes were committed with handguns.

Knives and Sharp Objects

According to the NCVS survey, an annual average of approximately 570,000 violent victimizations were committed with a knife or other sharp object. This figure accounts for about 6% of all violent crimes.

From 1993 through 2001, crimes involving knives or sharp objects were committed at an average annual rate of 3 per 1,000 persons age 12 or older. In 85% of these victimizations, about 482,000 annually, the weapon was a knife. In the remainder, about 88,000 victimizations per year on average, the weapon was another type of sharp object.

Blunt Objects

According to the NCVS survey, an annual average of approximately 356,000 violent crimes were committed by offenders armed with blunt objects such as bats, sticks, rocks, clubs, or blackjacks.

Other Weapons

According to the NCVS survey, about 5% of all violent crimes were committed with weapons other than guns, knives, or blunt objects. Such weapons include ropes, chains, poison, martial arts weapons, BB guns, and objects that could not be classified.

VICTIM CHARACTERIZATION

According to the NCVS survey, males, blacks, Hispanics, low-income individuals, and those aged 15 to 24 were more vulnerable to violent crime committed by armed assailants, in general, and firearm violence, in particular, than their respective counterparts, as follows:

Race/Ethnicity of Victim

For each type of weapon, victimization rates for whites were lower than those for blacks or Hispanics.

Armed Violence

The rate of armed violence for American Indians was 43% higher than the rate for blacks, 78% higher than the rate for Hispanics, and 184% higher than the rate for whites. An estimated 23% of white victims of violence, and 36% of black victims, were victims of violence involving an offender armed with a weapon.

Firearms

Blacks were victimized by offenders armed with guns at higher rates than Hispanics, but at similar rates as American Indians. The rate of firearm violence for blacks was more than twice that for whites whereas the rate for Hispanics was about twice that for whites. Approximately 7% of white victims and 17% of black victims were involved in incidents in which an offender was armed with a gun.

Firearm violence rates for blacks aged 12 or older were 40% higher than rates for Hispanics, and 200% higher than rates for whites. In fact, blacks were about 9 times more likely than whites to be victims of gun-related homicides. Blacks accounted for 49% of homicide victims and 54% of victims of firearm homicide. This is so even though blacks represent only 12% of the U.S. population.

Knives, Blunt Objects and Other Weapons

Blacks had similar victimization rates as Hispanics for crimes committed with knives or blunt objects/other weapons.

Unarmed Violence

No significant differences separated the rates at which whites and blacks were victimized by unarmed offenders.

Age of Victim

Approximately forty-five percent of all violence with a weapon involved victims between ages 25 and 49, and 38% involved victims between ages 15 and 24. For overall violence, persons age 12-14, 15-17, and 18-20 were victimized at similar rates, higher than those for persons age 21 or older. The rates of violent victimization, violent victimization involving a weapon, and violent victimization involving a firearm for persons age 18-20 were approximately 20 times those of persons age 65 or older.

Both for crimes committed with any weapon and for firearm violence specifically, differences between black and Hispanic victimization rates were greatest within the age category 18-20. Whites and blacks, aged 18-20, were more likely than whites and blacks of other ages to have been victims of weapon violence in general, and firearm violence in particular.

Hispanics aged 15-17 and 18-20 were more vulnerable than other Hispanics to violence involving a weapon, and violence involving a firearm.

For blacks, whites, and Hispanics, victims of violent crime were, on average, younger than the general population. For the general population as well as for the victim population, the mean age of whites was greater than the mean age of blacks.

Overall among the victims, blacks were older than Hispanics, the youngest racial or ethnic group considered. This pattern of relative ages was true for victims of violence involving firearms.

A table setting forth the type of weapon used, by age of victim, from 1993 to 2001, is set forth at Appendix 1.

Murder of Children Under age 12

Weapons in general, and firearms specifically, were less commonly used against murder victims under age 12 than against those age 12 or older. From 1993 through 2001, about 2 in 5 murders of children under age 12 involved a weapon, and about 1 in 6 involved a firearm whereas among victims age 12 or older, 91% of the murders were committed with a weapon, and 70% were committed with a firearm.

In 1993, firearms accounted for 19% of murders of children under age 12. This peak of 195 incidents preceded a decline in 2001, when 15% of all such murders, amounting to 127 of 824 murders, involved a firearm.

A table setting forth the murder rate of children under age 12, by weapon used from 1993 to 2001, is set forth at Appendix 2.

Armed Violence

Vulnerability to victimization by an armed offender similarly varied by the age of victim. Younger persons, particularly those age 18-20, had higher rates of victimization by armed offenders.

Firearms

The rate of firearm violence was also highest for persons age 18-20. Their rate was about 40% higher than the rate for persons ages 15 to 17 and 21 to 24. Except for victims age 12-14, for whom firearm violence constituted about 3% of all violent crime, firearm violence accounted for between 9% and 13% of all violent crime for each age group. On average, black victims of firearm violence were 3 years younger than white victims.

Knives, Sharp Objects and Other Weapons

Crimes committed with knives or other sharp objects accounted for 6% to 8% of all violent crime for each age group, whereas crimes with other weapons accounted for 9% to 11% of all violent crime for each age group examined.

Gender

According to the NCVS survey, approximately 1 in 3 male victims of violent crime were confronted by an armed offender whereas about 1 in 5 female victims of violent crime faced an armed assailant. This pattern was generally consistent across weapon types, i.e., for each type of weapon, the victimization rate for males was about twice that for females.

Eight in ten male homicide victims were killed with a firearm, compared to 6 in 10 female victims. Knives or other sharp objects were the second most frequently used weapon in homicides of both males and females.

Males were 5 times more likely than females to be a victim of a homicide committed with a firearm, and twice as likely to be murdered with a knife or other sharp object.

Annual household income

At almost every level of household income, blacks were more vulnerable than whites and Hispanics to violence involving a weapon and involving a firearm. Whites and blacks with household incomes below $7,500 were more vulnerable to armed violence than their counterparts with higher incomes.

In addition, persons with annual household incomes of less than $7,500 experienced both armed violence and firearm violence at about 3 times the rates of persons with annual household incomes of $50,000 or more.

For violence by an offender with a weapon and for violence by an offender armed with a gun, blacks with household incomes of less than $50,000 were victimized at rates higher than those of Hispanics or whites with similar incomes.

VICTIM-OFFENDER RELATIONSHIP

Crimes committed by intimates were less likely than crimes committed by strangers to involve a weapon. The offender was armed in one-sixth of all violence committed by an intimate and one-third of all violence by a stranger.

A table setting forth the weapon used, by victim/offender relationship type, from 1993 to 2001, is set forth at Appendix 3.

INJURIES SUFFERED

According to the NCVS survey, about 25% of violent crimes overall resulted in an injury to the victim, and crimes committed with weapons, and without weapons, were about equally likely to result in victim injury.

A table setting forth injuries suffered from violent victimizations, by type of weapon used, from 1993 to 2001, is set forth at Appendix 4.

Classification of Injuries

According to the NCVS survey, gunshot or knife wounds, broken bones, loss of teeth, internal injuries, loss of consciousness, and undetermined injuries requiring two or more days of hospitalization, were classified as serious injuries.

Injuries including bruises, black eyes, cuts, scratches, swelling, chipped teeth, and undetermined injuries requiring less than 2 days of hospitalization were classified as minor injuries.

The survey defined rape as sexual intercourse forced on the victim through physical or psychological coercion. Forced sexual intercourse includes vaginal, anal, or oral penetration by the offender, including penetration by a foreign object. Rape victims can be male or female, and the rape can be heterosexual or homosexual. The NCVS survey classifies completed rape as a serious injury.

For the purposes of the survey, rape without additional injury was categorized as an injury but not as a serious or minor injury. Cases in which the victim suffered additional injuries were grouped according to the severity of those additional injuries.

Armed Violence versus Unarmed Violence

According to the NCVS survey, crimes committed with weapons were about 3.5 times as likely to result in serious injury as crimes committed by unarmed offenders. Of all violence with a weapon, the crimes committed with blunt objects/other weapons were the most often associated with victim injury whereas 28% of crimes committed with knives or sharp objects, and 15% of crimes committed with firearms involved injury. For nonfatal violent crimes, offenders were more likely to have a firearm than a knife or club.

Injuries Suffered During Robbery

According to the survey, robbery is defined as a completed or attempted theft, directly from a person, of property or cash by force or threat of force, with or without a weapon, and with or without injury.

Robbery victims were more likely than assault victims to sustain injury. About half of victims of robbery by offenders armed with blunt objects or other weapons sustained an injury during the crime.

About a third of victims of robbery by unarmed offenders, and offenders armed with knives or sharp objects sustained injury during the victimization. Offenders armed with any weapon other than a firearm inflicted a serious injury during about 1 in 7 robberies that they committed.

Victims of robbery by offenders armed with blunt objects or other weapons were more likely than victims of robbery by offenders armed with a firearm to be attacked without a prior threat.

Injuries Suffered During Assault

According to the NCVS survey, simple assault is defined as an attack without a weapon resulting in either no injury or minor injury. Aggravated assault is defined as an attack or attempted attack with a weapon, regardless of whether an injury occurred, and attack without a weapon when serious injury results.

Victims were injured in one-third of all assaults by offenders armed with blunt objects or other weapons. Less than one-third of assaults by offenders armed with guns or knives resulted in injury. Victims of offenders armed with a knife or sharp object were the most likely to sustain a serious injury.

Injuries Suffered During Rape/Sexual Assault

According to the NCVS survey, rape is defined as forced sexual intercourse including both psychological coercion as well as physical force. Forced sexual intercourse includes vaginal, anal, or oral penetration by the offender or a foreign object. This category includes rapes of male and female victims, and both heterosexual and homosexual rape. Attempted rape includes verbal threats of rape.

Sexual assault is defined as a wide range of victimizations, separate from rape or attempted rape. These crimes include attacks or attempted attacks generally involving unwanted sexual contact between victim and offender. Sexual assaults may or may not involve force, and include such things as grabbing or fondling. Sexual assault also includes verbal threats.

About one-half of all victims of rape/sexual assault committed by unarmed offenders were injured, compared to three-quarters of victims of such crimes by armed offenders.

Injuries sustained included a completed rape. Because completed rape is considered an injury, victims of rape/sexual assault were more likely than robbery or assault victims to be injured, regardless of offender weapon use.

Homicide

Between 1993 and 2001, local law enforcement agencies reported 160,396 murders and nonnegligent manslaughters of persons age 12 or older. There was an annual average of 17,822 murders of persons age 12 or older.

A weapon was used in 91% of these crimes. Seventy percent of homicide victims were killed with a firearm. Handguns were used in 56% of all homicides.

In 4% of the homicides, the offender used a means such as strangling, punching, and kicking. Information about the weapon used was unavailable in 5% of all homicides.

Victim Self-Defense

According to the NCVS survey, about 61% of all victims of violent crime reported taking a self-defensive measure during the incident. Most used nonaggressive means, such as trying to escape, getting help, or attempting to scare off or warn the offender. About 13% of victims of violent crime tried to attack or threaten the offender. About 2% of victims of violent crime used a weapon to defend themselves. Of that number, one-half, amounting to 1% of violent crime victims, brandished a firearm.

A table setting forth the victims' methods of defense to violent crime, from 1993 to 2001, is set forth at Appendix 5.

LOCATION OF VICTIMIZATION

The most common locations for armed violence and gun violence were on the street. Thirty percent of violence with a weapon, and 35% of gun violence, occurred away from the victim's home. Twenty-seven percent of armed violence, and 25% of gun violence, occurred at or near the victim's home.

In addition, most violence involving a weapon, and most firearm violence, occurred while the victims were engaged in leisure activities away from home and commuting to work.

Approximately 6% of armed violence, and 2% of firearm violence occurred at a school or on school grounds. School violence is discussed in more detail in Chapter 7 of this almanac.

A table setting forth the type of weapon used, by victim's activity at time of incident, from 1993 to 2001, is set forth at Appendix 6.

TIME OF DAY

Violent crimes at night were more likely than crimes occurring during the day to involve a weapon. Three of every five crimes committed by an offender with a firearm occurred at night.

A table setting forth the type of weapon used, by time of day, from 1993 to 2001, is set forth at Appendix 7.

WEAPON USE AND TYPE OF CRIME

According to the NCVS survey, weapon use varied by type of crime. Robberies, followed by all assaults, were more likely to involve an armed assailant while rape/sexual assault was the least likely. Approximately 50%

of all robberies, 25% of all assaults, and one-twelfth of all rapes/sexual assaults involved an armed assailant.

Thirteen percent of robberies, 6% of assaults, and 3% of rapes were committed with a knife or other sharp object. Victims were confronted by offenders armed with guns in about 27% of robberies, 8% of assaults, and 3% of all rapes/sexual assaults.

In addition, about 90% of homicide victims were killed with a weapon.

A table setting forth the percentage of weapon use reported, by type of violent crime, from 1993 to 2001, is set forth at Appendix 8.

CRIME OUTCOME

According to the NCVS survey, whether the offender was armed or unarmed weighed heavily on crime outcome.

Robbery

Armed robberies were more likely to be completed, resulting in loss of property, than unarmed robberies. Higher completion percentages occurred for robberies committed with firearms than for robberies with knives and other sharp or blunt objects, or other weapons. Robberies committed with knives and unarmed robberies were completed at similar percentages.

Rape/Sexual Assault

The percentage of rapes/sexual assaults that were completed did not vary significantly depending on the offenders' possession of a weapon. About 71% of rapes/sexual assaults involving no weapon were completed whereas 67% of such assaults with a weapon were completed.

Assault

The outcome for incidents of assault was measured by whether a victim sustained an injury as a result of the crime. Overall, about 1 in 4 assault victims were injured during the incident. About 1 in 3 assault victims were injured when the offender possessed a blunt object or some unspecified type of weapon. About 1 in 4 victims were injured when the assailant had a knife. Victims of firearm violence were less likely than other victims to be injured.

CHAPTER 2:
PUNISHMENT

THE CRIMINAL JUSTICE SYSTEM

The criminal justice system refers to the organizations and individuals involved in protecting society from crime, and bringing criminals to justice. The goal of the criminal justice process is to adjudge the guilt or innocence of the accused. If he or she is found guilty, the criminal justice system is responsible for punishing and/or rehabilitating the criminal.

The criminal justice process begins following the commission of a crime once it is reported to law enforcement authorities. Once an arrest is made, and charges are filed against the criminal, the crime is considered "a crime against the state." The prosecuting attorney represents the interests of the state against the criminal, and only indirectly does he or she represent the interests of the victim.

The crime victim, who has already been devastated by their misfortune, often confronts the criminal justice system with great apprehension, as they attempt to seek justice. It is therefore important that the crime victim develop a basic knowledge of the organizations that compose the criminal justice system, the individuals who are involved in the process, and the basic procedures followed in bringing an offender to justice.

The criminal justice system can be broken down into four basic segments according to the role they play in apprehending, prosecuting and punishing the criminal, including (i) law enforcement; (ii) the prosecutor; (iii) the court; and (iv) corrections, as further discussed below.

THE ROLE OF LAW ENFORCEMENT

Law enforcement officials generally make the first contact with the crime victim following the commission of the crime. It is the responsibility of the law enforcement official to investigate the crime, gather evidence, and apprehend and arrest the offender. Once arrested, the criminal is usually taken by the law enforcement official to jail to be identified, fingerprinted and booked, and to await further processing. The law enforcement officer may also be responsible for conducting follow-up investigations, and to testify in the criminal proceedings.

If the victim witnessed the crime, he or she may be asked by the police to cooperate in the investigation. For example, the victim may be asked to try and identify the perpetrator. This may be accomplished by looking through books which contain photographs of the criminal. These photographs are known as "mug shots." In addition, the victim may be asked to view a lineup to see if he or she can identify the perpetrator in person. A lineup consists of a number of individuals who are viewed by the victim through a one-way mirror. The individuals may be asked to repeat certain words which were spoken during the commission of the crime.

There are a number of other ways a victim may be asked to cooperate, such as wearing a "wire" to record incriminating conversations. Of course, such requests carry a certain amount of risk to the victim, and are not typically sought. In any event, a victim is never forced to cooperate with law enforcement. However, as a practical matter, without such cooperation it is less likely that the crime will ever be solved and the criminal apprehended and brought to justice.

THE ROLE OF THE PROSECUTOR

The prosecutor is responsible for representing the people of the jurisdiction in bringing the offender to justice. It is the prosecutor's decision whether or not to prosecute a particular case after reviewing all of the facts. The prosecutor participates at every stage of the criminal proceedings, including the arraignment and bail determination, any preliminary hearings, the trial, and the sentencing phase.

THE ROLE OF THE COURT

The criminal proceedings are presided over by a criminal court judge, who is responsible for overseeing the proceedings, and making certain rulings. For example, the judge generally decides whether bail will be granted to the offender, and determines the acceptability of a plea bargain arrangement proposed by the prosecutor and defense attorney. In addition, the judge decides the offender's punishment, such as the sentence to be served.

THE ROLE OF THE CORRECTIONS DEPARTMENT

After the criminal has been sentenced, it is the role of the corrections department to make sure that sentence is carried out. This may include supervision during a period of probation, incarceration or parole.

Probation

Probation refers to the period of time during which a convicted criminal must be supervised in lieu of incarceration, i.e., the sentence is suspended. Probation is usually awarded when the offender has little or no criminal history, and is not a danger to society.

An individual known as a probation officer is usually assigned to supervise the convict during his or her period of probation. The court may place certain conditions on the probation, such as the payment of certain fines, or participation in counseling. If the convict fails to comply with these conditions, probation may be revoked and the convict incarcerated for the remainder of the sentence.

Incarceration

If the convicted criminal is sentenced to a period of imprisonment, he or she is placed under the supervision of the prison staff. The prison staff is responsible for maintaining the security of the institution. The prison also provides the convict with educational opportunities, counseling, and job training, as well as medical care when required.

Parole

Parole refers to the period of time during which a convicted criminal must be supervised, upon release from prison after having served a portion of his or her sentence. The decision to parole the convict is made by the parole board after a hearing. The crime victim is entitled to attend the parole hearing, and to prepare a victim impact statement concerning his or her position concerning the convict's early release.

If parole is granted, the parole board generally places certain conditions upon the paroled convict. The convict is supervised in the community by an individual known as a parole officer. If the paroled convict violates the conditions of parole, he or she is returned to prison to serve the remainder of the original sentence.

THE JUVENILE OFFENDER

Unfortunately, many violent crimes are committed by the nation's youth. The juvenile court, also known as the family court in some jurisdictions, was established to handle cases involving children up to a statutorily defined age. The majority of states have designated age 18 as the upper limit, although some states limit jurisdiction to age 16.

A child who commits a crime and is processed through the juvenile court system is adjudicated delinquent and receives more lenient treatment due to his or her minority. The trend is towards rehabilitation rather than punishment, in an effort to save these children before they are able to turn into adult criminals.

Depending on the severity of the crime, the juvenile court judge can seek transfer of a delinquency case to an adult criminal court and, in some states, the juvenile court is bypassed and the adult criminal court is automatically given jurisdiction over certain crimes. The trend among the states has been to make it easier for juvenile offenders to be treated as adults. In fact, many states have enacted legislation which requires automatic transfer to adult criminal court in cases involving serious or violent offenses, and all states now allow adult criminal prosecution of juveniles in certain circumstances.

More detailed information on the juvenile justice system may be found in this author's legal almanac entitled *Your Child's Legal Rights: An Overview*, also published by Oceana Publishing Company.

THE DEATH PENALTY

The death penalty is a punishment reserved for the most heinous crimes. Once banned in the United States as cruel and unusual punishment, the death penalty—also known as capital punishment—returned to America in 1976 when the Supreme Court lifted its ban after a number of states rewrote their death penalty statutes to satisfy concerns over the arbitrary application of the punishment. The Federal Government has also statutorily authorized the death penalty for a number of offenses.

Although the specific death penalty provisions of state statutes vary greatly, the typical statute now requires a bifurcated trial in capital cases, i.e. one which is divided into two components. During the first stage, the jury determines guilt or innocence. If the defendant is judged innocent, the trial is over. If the defendant is found guilty, the trial proceeds to its second stage at which point the jury—or in some states, the judge—chooses imprisonment or death in light of any aggravating or mitigating circumstances.

Nearly all state capital punishment statutes differ with respect to which crimes constitute capital offenses. For example, some states—such as Delaware—limit the death penalty to first degree murder, while other states—such as Arkansas—may hand down a death sentence for a number of other crimes, such as treason.

Following are the methods that have been used to carry out this punishment: (i) hanging; (ii) firing squad; (iii) electrocution; (iv) lethal gas; and (v) lethal injection. The majority of states now use lethal injection as the preferred method of execution. The manner of execution in Federal death penalty cases is the method employed by the state in which the federal sentence is handed down. The U.S. Military has its own death penalty statute, which employs lethal injection as the manner of execution.

Presently, sixteen states permit the death penalty for juvenile offenders who are younger than 18 years of age. In 14 states, the death penalty may not be imposed unless the offender is 18 or older. The federal government also specifies age 18 as the minimum age for a death penalty sentence.

More detailed information on the death penalty may be found in this author's legal almanac entitled *The Law of Capital Punishment*, also published by Oceana Publishing Company.

CHAPTER 3:
VIOLENCE AGAINST CHILDREN

IN GENERAL

It is a sad fact that children are often the innocent victims of crimes perpetrated against them by both family members and strangers. Children have been subjected to violent acts of child abuse, including sexual abuse and murder. Children have been abducted, raped, and introduced to the deviant world of child pornography and prostitution. According to the United States Department of Health and Human Services, each year, almost 3 million children are alleged to have been abused or neglected, and nearly 1 million are found to have been victims of some type of maltreatment.

A resource directory for child victims of violence is set forth at Appendix 9.

CHILD ABUSE

Child abuse occurs when physical injury is inflicted upon, or permitted to be inflicted upon, a child, by his or her parent or legal guardian. Statutes have generally defined physical child abuse as punching, beating, kicking, biting, burning, or otherwise harming a child.

In some cases, serious injuries may be unintentionally inflicted upon a child as a result of excessive physical punishment. Although physical discipline by a parent is permitted in all states, it must be reasonable and not excessive. The "reasonableness" standard is largely dependent on the age of the child. Of course, no matter how difficult a child may act, a parent is never permitted to cause serious physical injury to the child.

The factors within a family setting which are known to contribute to child abuse include (i) drug and/or alcohol abuse; (ii) poverty; (iii) lack of education; (iv) lack of parenting skills; (v) broken families; and (vi) domestic abuse. In addition, studies show that parents who were victims of abuse as children often repeat this behavior with their own children. Further, parents who suffer from drug or alcohol addiction are more likely to abuse their children. Abuse has also been found to exist to a greater degree when the home environment is under stress, such as a single-parent household, or a household suffering from depressed financial conditions.

Profile of an Abused Child

Behavioral

Although one or more of the following behaviors may occasionally be found in a child who is not abused or neglected, they are behaviors which are often found in such children, and should not be overlooked:

1. Extreme aggressiveness;

2. Anxiety;

3. Depression;

4. Fearfulness;

5. Habitual hunger;

6. Immaturity;

7. Lack of confidence;

8. Low self-esteem;

9. Self-hatred;

10. Sexual sophistication; and/or

11. Withdrawal.

Physical

The physical indications of abuse or neglect are more readily discernible, and may include one or more of the following:

1. A habitually unkempt appearance;

2. Bruises, cuts, burns, welts, bites, etc., for which there is no reasonable explanation, particularly if there appears to be a continuing pattern of the same types of injuries;

3. Sexually transmitted disease; and/or

4. Pregnancy.

Mandatory Reporting of Child Abuse

Every state has a statute which requires the reporting of known, as well as suspected, incidents of child abuse. Generally, professionals who come in contact with children are obligated to report suspected child abuse or neglect, or face criminal and civil penalties. They are referred to as mandatory reporters and include:

1. Medical or hospital personnel, such as doctors, dentists, nurses, and specialists;

2. Law enforcement personnel, such as police officers;

3. Social services personnel, such as social workers;

4. School personnel, such as teachers and guidance counselors;

5. Mental health professionals, such as psychiatrists and psychologists;

6. Child care providers.

All persons who suspect that a child is being abused or neglected may make a report to the appropriate authorities. In fact, in many states, ordinary citizens are also required by statute to report suspected child abuse or neglect.

The agency responsible for investigating child abuse or neglect reports is required to respond to a report within a specified amount of time after the report is received. If it is determined that a child has been abused, neglected, or is in an unsafe environment, the child may be taken into protective custody while an investigation is undertaken. In addition, where child abuse is documented, a report will generally be kept on file in the state's child abuse registry. The registry serves as a screening device to prevent perpetrators from being accepted into employment or caregiving situations where they will have extensive contact with children.

CHILD SEXUAL ABUSE

The sexual abuse of a child refers to forced, tricked, or coerced sexual behavior between a young person and an older person. It includes rape, pedophilia, child prostitution and pornography, and incest. Child sexual abuse has been defined by the U.S. Department of Health and Human Services to include "fondling a child's genitals, intercourse, incest, rape, sodomy, exhibitionism and the sexual exploitation of a child."

Child victims of sexual exploitation and sexual abuse, in general, come from a wide variety of family backgrounds, including all socioeconomic classes and religions. They range in age from infancy through adolescence. Many crave adult affection, and are lured into the behavior to obtain approval by adult authority figures.

Although children are continually warned not to speak to strangers, this admonition may not protect a child from becoming a victim of sexual abuse, because young children are often victimized by someone they already know and trust. The abuser may be a family member, a neighbor, a teacher, a coach, or as recent headlines have demonstrated, even a member of the clergy.

In fact, this is how intrafamilial sexual abuse can persist in secrecy. Since the child has a trusting and loving relationship with the abuser, he or she may naively believe that the adult is acting appropriately. Alternatively, in many cases there are threats of retaliation if the child reveals the abuse, and the child submits out of fear.

In recent years, there has been an attempt to recognize and deal with the problem of child sexual abuse, although the reported cases likely represent only a small fraction of the incidence of child sexual abuse. Studies show that girls are three times more likely to be sexually abused than boys, however, boys are more likely to suffer serious injury or death as a result. A large study of female adults found that sexual abuse of girls generally began at age 6 and lasted approximately 7 years. The perpetrator in more than half of those cases was the child's own biological father. Boys, however, are more likely to be abused by males outside of the family.

In addition, there is an increased awareness of the potential for child sexual abuse to occur in institutional settings, such as schools or day care centers. As a result, most states require the employer to conduct a criminal history background check of employees and applicants for employment in child care facilities and other institutions. Many of these laws allow only for a check of the convictions in a person's record, but others also include a check for prior arrests, and whether the applicant is known by the state's sex offender registry.

The long-term effects on children who have been victims of sexual abuse are devastating. They are generally unable to form normal sexual relationships with persons of the opposite sex. Many child victims fall into destructive lifestyles, such as drug and alcohol addiction, and many succumb to suicide.

Child Rape

According to studies conducted by the Bureau of Justice Statistics, approximately one-half of female rape victims are under 18 years old, and sixteen percent are younger than 12 years old. One study found that 96 percent of female rape victims younger than 12 years old knew their attackers and only 4 percent of those children were attacked by strangers. Fifty percent of the perpetrators were friends or acquaintances, and 46 percent were family members. In fact, twenty percent of the children were victimized by their fathers.

BJS studies also indicate that as the age of the female increases, rape by a family member decreases dramatically, while the incidence of rape by a stranger rises. For example, among female victims aged 12 to 17, 20 percent were raped by family members, 65 percent by an acquaintance or friend and 15 percent by a stranger. Among female victims age 18 years or older, 12 percent were raped by a family member, 55 percent by an acquaintance or friend, and 33 percent by a stranger.

Child Pornography

Child pornography and prostitution are highly organized, multimillion dollar industries that operate in our society on a nationwide scale. In 1977, Congressional hearings were held on the subject of child pornography, also known as "kiddie porn." Witnesses who appeared before Congress told nightmare tales about small children who were kidnapped by pornographers, or sold to pornographers by their parents.

Outraged federal and state legislators have since attempted to enact laws to combat this widespread problem. Following the Congressional hearings, two federal statutes were passed. The Protection of Children from Sexual Exploitation Act prohibits the production of any sexually explicit material using a child under the age of sixteen, if such material is destined for, or has already traveled in interstate commerce. In response to allegations that children were being sold by their parents into the pornography industry, the law was made applicable to parents or other custodians who knowingly permit a child to participate in the production of sexually explicit material.

Greater enforcement was subsequently obtained by enacting The Child Pornography Protection Act, which eliminated the requirement that child pornography distribution be undertaken for the purpose of "sale," and raised the age of protection to eighteen. In addition, penalties were greatly increased for violations of the Act, and a provision for criminal and civil forfeiture was included.

The text of the Child Pornography Protection Act of 1996 is set forth at Appendix 10.

Sex Offender Registration and Community Notification

In general, sex offender registration and community notification systems assist the investigation of sex crimes by informing law enforcement authorities of the identities and whereabouts of convicted sex offenders. These systems may also inhibit offenders—who know that the authorities know who they are and where they are—from committing additional crimes. Community notification enables communities to take common sense measures to protect themselves and their families, such as ensuring that their children do not associate or visit with known child molesters.

As set forth below, the United States Department of Justice (DOJ) has implemented a number of provisions designed to stop sex offenders before they strike. In addition, the DOJ has participated in state and federal litigation defending the validity of sex offender registration and notification systems in a number of jurisdictions.

The Jacob Wetterling Crimes Against Children and Sexually Violent Offender Registration Act

The Jacob Wetterling Crimes Against Children and Sexually Violent Offender Registration Act ("The Jacob Wetterling Act") provides states with a monetary incentive to adopt effective registration systems for convicted child molesters and other persons convicted of sexually violent crimes. Under the Act, community notification concerning the location of registered offenders is permitted where necessary for public safety. Most states have some form of sex offender registration but few regularly verify an offender's address. The Jacob Wetterling guidelines assist state law enforcement agencies in their communication with each other regarding sex offenders who cross state lines.

The full text of the Jacob Wetterling Act is set forth at Appendix 11.

Megan's Law

Over 40 states have passed laws requiring the registration of sexual offenders with state agencies. This type of law has commonly been referred to as "Megan's Law," named after a child who was sexually assaulted and murdered by a convicted sexual offender who was living in her neighborhood in anonymity. In 1994, seven-year-old Megan Kanka was sexually assaulted and murdered by a twice-convicted sex offender who moved in across the street from her family's home in New Jersey. The offender promised to show Megan his new puppy, luring her into his home where he raped and murdered her. Megan's body was subsequently found nearby.

"Megan's Law" was designed to strengthen the provisions of the Jacob Wetterling Act. Prior to the passage of Megan's Law, Section 170101(d) of the Jacob Wetterling Act provided that the information collected under a state sex offender registration program would be treated as private data except: (i) for disclosure to law enforcement agencies for law enforcement purposes; (ii) for disclosure to government agencies conducting confidential background checks; and (iii) that the designated state law enforcement agency and any local law enforcement agency authorized by the state shall release relevant information that is necessary to protect the public concerning a specific person required to register.

Megan's Law amended Section 170101(d) to provide that the information collected under a state sex offender registration program may be disclosed: (i) for any purpose permitted under the laws of the state; and (ii) that the designated state law enforcement agency and any local law enforcement agency authorized by the state shall release relevant information that is necessary to protect the public concerning a specific person required to register.

Thus, "Megan's Law" did away with the section that treated sex offender registration information as private, paving the way for states to publish this information to the community.

"Megan's Law," basically requires that neighbors, community officials, organizations and individuals working with potential victims of sex offenders, e.g. children, or those likely to come in contact with the sex offender, be notified that the convicted sex offender is living amongst them. In addition, sex offenders are required to register with a state agency in order to keep track of their behavior and whereabouts.

The full text of Megan's Law is set forth at Appendix 12.

CHILD ABDUCTION

In an effort to combat child abduction, most states have adopted laws relating to missing children. For example, many states now require that a missing child's school records and birth certificate be flagged in some way. Schools often require a child's birth certificate and/or prior school records in order to register the child. Thus, if the abductor tries to register the child, and the abductor cannot produce these records, the school will be alerted to the whereabouts of the missing child.

The AMBER Plan

The AMBER Plan was created in 1996 in memory of Amber Hagerman, a 9-year old girl who was kidnapped and brutally murdered while riding her bicycle in Arlington, Texas. The community was so outraged that they contacted the local radio stations and requested that alerts be transmitted on-air whenever a child is missing to help find the abducted child. Statistics indicate that time is the most important factor in recovering an abducted child. Amber's name was used as an acronym to stand for "America's Missing: Broadcast Emergency Response."

The AMBER Plan is a voluntary partnership between law enforcement agencies and broadcasters to activate an urgent bulletin in the most serious child abduction cases. Broadcasters use the Emergency Alert System (EAS) to broadcast a description of the abducted child and suspected abductor. The goal of the AMBER Alert is to instantly galvanize the entire community to assist in the search for and safe return of the child.

As soon as law enforcement is notified that a child has been abducted, they must first make sure that the case meets the AMBER Plan criteria for triggering the alert. Although that criteria may vary depending on the jurisdiction, the National Center for Missing & Exploited Children suggests three criteria that should be met before an Alert is activated.

1. Law enforcement confirms a child has been abducted;

2. Law enforcement believes the circumstances surrounding the abduction indicate that the child is in danger of serious bodily harm or death;

3. There is enough descriptive information about the child, abductor, and/or suspect's vehicle to believe an immediate broadcast alert will help.

If these criteria are met, the information must be quickly put together for public distribution and faxed to radio stations designated as primary stations under the Emergency Alert System. The primary stations in turn send the information to area radio, television and cable systems to be broadcast to listeners. Radio stations generally interrupt programming to announce the alert while television and cable systems place the alert across the bottom of the screen. Some states also display the alert on their electronic highway billboards and include information about the abducted child, the abductor, and/or the suspected vehicle if one is involved in the abduction.

CHAPTER 4:
VIOLENCE AGAINST THE ELDERLY

IN GENERAL

Elderly people have often been targeted as victims of crime, largely due to their frailty and inability to adequately defend themselves. However, as the baby boom generation moves towards senior citizenship, this group constitutes a much larger segment of society, and thus draws more attention than ever before.

The National Center for Elder Abuse is a federal grant-funded partnership of leading organizations involved with preventing elder abuse. The organization provides comprehensive information about elder abuse, including hotline reporting numbers, elder abuse laws, and other helpful information and resources for the elderly victim of violence.

A resource directory for elderly victims of violence is set forth at Appendix 13.

Because senior citizens represent a powerful political block which politicians can no longer ignore, more effective legislation has been enacted to protect the elderly from abuse, as further discussed below. In addition, there are a number of governmental and private organizations that endeavor to protect the rights of the elderly, and the reader is advised to contact these organizations for additional information.

A directory of state offices for the aging is set forth at Appendix 14; a directory of national organizations for the elderly is set forth at Appendix 15; and a directory of national legal services for the elderly is set forth at Appendix 16.

THE ELDERLY VICTIM

Due to their relative inability to protect themselves, the elderly are subjected to types of crimes which prey upon their weaknesses. For example, the elderly are particularly susceptible to crimes motivated by financial gain, such as muggings, robberies, and burglaries.

For example, robbery constitutes 38% of the violent crimes against the elderly versus only 20% of the violence experienced by persons younger than age 65. Elderly victims of robbery and theft are more likely than younger victims to report those crimes to law enforcement officials.

The elderly are much more likely to be victimized at or near their home. This is due to the fact that many senior citizens live alone, are unemployed, and spend most of their time in their homes or the immediate neighborhood. Consequently, fear of leaving their home, particularly after dark, is a common concern among senior citizens.

Elderly victims are vulnerable, and are less likely to act in their own defense than younger victims. Older victims generally do not take any type of physical action against their perpetrator, and are less likely to resist. In addition, elderly men generally have higher victimization rates than elderly women although elderly women are more susceptible to personal thefts, such as muggings and purse snatchings.

The typical—and most susceptible—elderly victim has the following characteristics:

1. Age range of 65 to 74;

2. Minority;

3. Urban center resident;

4. Separated or divorced; and

5. Apartment dweller.

Further, the elderly in lower income brackets experience higher violence rates, and elderly in higher income brackets experience more economic crimes.

DOMESTIC ELDER ABUSE

"Domestic elder abuse" refers to crimes against the elderly committed by family members or caregivers, which generally occurs within the victim's home. This abuse often takes place at the hands of spouses and adult children. It is reported that alcohol consumption is a substantial factor in such abuse. In these scenarios, the majority of the abusers as well as victims are female. State reports have shown a dramatic increase of 206% in elder abuse and neglect since 1987.

NURSING HOME ABUSE

It is a sad and unfortunate fact that many elderly residents of nursing homes have been subjected to criminal acts of abuse. Violent acts of nursing home abuse include physical abuse, such as assault and battery; sexual assault and battery, including sexual molestation and rape; and corporal punishment.

Federal and state laws provide that a resident in a nursing home has the right to be free from physical, sexual, and mental abuse, as well as involuntary seclusion. In addition, there are federal and state regulations aimed at preventing the employment of individuals who have been convicted of abuse, neglect or maltreatment in a health care setting.

There are a number of agencies that should be contacted if a nursing home resident is subjected to abuse, including the local law enforcement officials; the state office of aging; the state long-term care ombudsman; the state licensing and certification agency; and the state's adult protective services office.

Physical Abuse

Physical abuse is the intentional use of physical force upon an individual that is likely to result in bodily injury or pain. Physical abuse in the nursing home setting occurs when a staff member or co-resident physically assaults the resident. This may include but is not limited to hitting, punching, shoving, slapping, kicking, burning, shaking, or force-feeding the resident.

In the nursing home setting, physical abuse is extremely serious due to the often fragile condition of the elderly residents. Elderly people are more susceptible to fractures because their bones are generally more brittle. In addition, the thinness and lack of elasticity in their skin causes them to bruise and cut more easily.

Indications that a nursing home resident may be the victim of physical abuse include unexplained black eyes; sprains; fractures; cuts and bruises; internal bleeding; and hair loss. In addition, if a family member is denied access to the resident, this should raise a warning signal that something may be wrong. In such a case, carefully examine the resident and watch for any unusual change in the resident's behavior, such as anxiety, fear or stress, particularly if there is a strong reaction to certain nursing home employees or co-residents.

Be aware that if the resident does not admit to being victimized, he or she may fear retaliation from the abusive staff member. It may take some time to convince the victim that they do not have anything to fear. Once the abuse has been confirmed, immediately contact local law enforcement authorities and obtain medical help.

If you suspect that the resident has been the victim of physical abuse, and there is evidence of possible abuse, but he or she will not admit it, or is unable to communicate effectively, law enforcement should still be called and the person should be taken for medical evaluation. If you are not sure whether abuse has occurred, you should still confidentially convey your suspicions to the nursing home administrator, and ask that the situation be monitored.

Sexual Abuse

Sexual abuse in the nursing home setting generally involves any type of nonconsensual sexual contact, including improper touching and forced sexual acts, such as rape and sodomy. Sadly, elderly nursing home residents fall victim to sexual abuse because of their fragility and inability to defend themselves. In addition, many nursing home residents are unable to effectively communicate, making them easy prey for sexual predators, including staff members and co-residents.

Indications that a nursing home resident may be the victim of sexual abuse include unexplained bruising in the genital area, buttocks or breasts; difficulty walking or sitting; vaginal and/or anal bleeding; genital infections, irritation or injury; sexually transmitted diseases; and torn or bloody undergarments. Again, carefully examine the resident and watch for any unusual change in the resident's behavior, such as anxiety, fear or stress, particularly if there is a strong reaction to certain nursing home employees or co-residents.

As with suspected physical abuse described above, if there are indications of sexual abuse, law enforcement authorities must be notified and the resident must be taken for medical evaluation and treatment, whether or not the resident admits that sexual abuse has taken place.

Nursing Home Liability for Abuse

Under the law, nursing home residents have the right to be free from physical, sexual and emotional abuse. Nursing homes have a duty to thoroughly investigate the background of the employees it hires. In addition, if the investigation reveals that an applicant has criminal convictions that would indicate their unsuitability for working in the nursing home setting, including convictions for crimes such as child abuse or sexual assault, the nursing home has an obligation to report that individual.

When abuse occurs, the nursing home itself may be liable for the conduct of the offending staff member if:

1. The nursing home failed to conduct an adequate background investigation which would have revealed a staff member's propensity for violence or sexual assault.

2. The nursing home was understaffed and failed to employ a sufficient number of employees to supervise the staff and residents.

3. The nursing home failed to properly train its employees concerning physical, sexual and mental abuse.

4. The nursing home failed to properly supervise its employees.

5. The nursing home continued to employ a person who exhibited signs of aggression or improper sexual tendencies towards residents.

LEGISLATION

In an effort to deter crimes against elderly victims, and to express society's intolerance toward such behavior, many state legislatures have created special classes of offenses involving crimes against the elderly. Many states provide that crimes committed against the elderly carry harsher penalties.

A table of state statutes concerning elder abuse is set forth at Appendix 17.

In addition, federal and state legislation is being passed which provides special protection and privileges to elderly victims of crime. For example, most crime victim compensation statutes require a minimum financial loss—e.g. $100—to be eligible for relief. Due to the realization that many senior citizens survive on fixed incomes, this minimum loss requirement is generally waived for the elderly victim.

Further, legislators have enacted mandatory reporting requirements concerning elder abuse which requires certain designated mandatory reporters—such as health care providers—to report suspected elder abuse or neglect. The reporter is required to report the incident or risk penalty for failure to report.

States have also enacted laws to deal with the special needs of elderly victims who must participate in the criminal justice system. For example, crimes involving elderly victims often receive a trial preference, i.e., priority scheduling on the trial calendar. In addition, some states permit an elderly victim to testify by alternate methods—e.g., by videotape or closed circuit television—as opposed to coming into court. Further, being mindful of diminished visual and auditory senses, most states accommodate elderly victims by providing enlarged visuals and sound amplification devices.

CHAPTER 5:
VIOLENCE AGAINST WOMEN

IN GENERAL

According to the U.S. Department of Justice, Bureau of Justice Statistics (BJS), women are the victims of more than 4.5 million violent crimes each year. This alarming figure includes approximately 500,000 rapes or other sexual assaults. In addition, this figure may not accurately reflect the rate of violence against women because many women are reluctant to report a number of violent crimes to law enforcement authorities, including sexual assaults and offenses committed by intimates. There is a general belief that no purpose would be served by reporting these crimes. Sexual attacks, in particular, are perceived as too personal to reveal, and many women feel that the subsequent investigation subjects them to additional trauma.

More detailed information on violence against women may be found in this author's legal almanac entitled *The Law of Violence Against Women*, also published by Oceana Publishing Company.

A resource directory for women victims of violence is set forth at Appendix 18.

THE VIOLENCE AGAINST WOMEN ACT

The Violence Against Women Act ("VAWA") was enacted as part of the Violent Crime Control and Law Enforcement Act of 1994 (the "Crime Bill"). The VAWA is landmark bipartisan legislation which sets forth firm law enforcement tactics and includes important safeguards for female victims of sexual assault and domestic violence.

Following is an outline of the most important aspects of the VAWA:

Subtitle A: The Safe Streets for Women Act

The Safe Streets for Women Act provides for stiffer federal penalties for repeat sex crime offenders; authorizes mandatory restitution enforceable by victims of sex crimes; and provides funding to the U.S. Attorney's Office for the purpose of hiring federal victim/witness counselors in connection with the prosecution of sex and domestic violence crimes. The Act also makes an important amendment to the Federal Rules of Evidence, limiting inquiries into a victim's past sexual behavior or predisposition, and ensuring the confidentiality of communications between victims and their counselors.

Subtitle B: The Safe Homes for Women Act

The Safe Homes For Women Act provides for interstate enforcement of domestic violence offenses, making it a crime to cross state lines to continue to abuse a spouse or partner; and authorizes mandatory restitution enforceable by victims of domestic violence. The Act also provides that protection orders are entitled to full faith and credit by the courts of another jurisdiction with the same enforceability as if that jurisdiction had issued the order, and provides for the confidentiality of domestic violence shelters and the addresses of abuse victims. The Act further implements programs designed to educate young people about domestic violence and provides funding for a National Domestic Violence Hotline.

Subtitle C: The Civil Rights Remedies for Gender-Motivated Violence Act

The Civil Rights Remedies for Gender-Motivated Violence Act establishes a Federal civil rights cause of action for victims of crimes of violence motivated by gender, and authorizes attorney's fees for the victim. This civil rights remedy was designed to complement existing federal civil rights laws which do not protect women from gender-motivated violence. Under the Act, victims of gender-motivated violent crimes, such as rape and domestic violence, now have the right to sue their attackers for damages under federal law.

Subtitle D: The Equal Justice for Women in the Courts Act

The Equal Justice for Women in the Courts Act provides monetary grants for the purpose of developing programs for training judges and court personnel about sexual assault, domestic violence and other crimes of violence motivated by gender.

Subtitle E: Violence Against Women Act Improvements

The Violence Against Women Act Improvements section strengthens the provisions of the Act by providing for pre-trial detention in sex offense cases; increasing penalties against victims below the age of 16; requiring payment for the cost of testing victims for sexually transmitted diseases in sex offense cases; requiring defendants in sex offense cases to be tested for HIV/AIDS disease; strengthening the restitution provisions by enforcing restitution orders through suspension of the defendants' federal benefits; and providing for studies on campus sexual assault and battered women's syndrome.

Subtitle F: National Stalker and Domestic Violence Reduction

The National Stalker and Domestic Violence Reduction section authorizes access to federal criminal information databases for use in domestic violence or stalking cases; and provides monetary grants to States and local governmental units to improve methods of entering data regarding stalking and domestic violence incidents into local, State and national crime information databases.

Stalking is discussed more fully in Chapter 6 of this almanac.

THE DEPARTMENT OF JUSTICE VIOLENCE AGAINST WOMEN OFFICE

The Violence Against Women Office is responsible for the overall coordination and focus of Department of Justice efforts to combat violence against women, serving as the primary point of contact for other federal agencies, state and local governments, outside organizations, and Congress. The goal of the Violence Against Women Office is to promote greater awareness of the problem of violence against women, and to find effective solutions.

SEXUAL ASSAULT

Sexual assault is a general term which refers to a number of sex-related offenses, including rape, sexual contact, and indecent exposure. Sexual assault involves the commission of those acts against another who is either unwilling to consent, or who lacks the physical, mental or legal capacity to consent, e.g. a minor. The crime of sexual assault almost always involves sexual intercourse, including oral or anal intercourse, or some other type of penetration of the genitals by another's body or by an object.

Sexual violence against children is discussed in Chapter 3 of this almanac.

The profile of the most likely victim of rape or sexual assault is a female, between the ages of 16 and 19, who lives in an urban center and comes from a low income household. Although the victims of sexual assault are primarily female, many states have recently amended their laws to make such crimes gender-neutral.

In prosecuting a sexual assault case, the issue of consent is of primary importance. If the victim was acquainted with the offender—e.g. date rape—it often becomes a matter of credibility unless there is further corroborating evidence, such as witnesses. However, some states have passed laws prohibiting law enforcement officers from requiring the victim of a sexual assault to submit to a polygraph test as a condition of beginning the criminal investigation.

In addition, most states no longer require evidence that the victim attempted to physically resist the attacker, and in all 50 states, it is now a crime to sexually assault one's spouse.

Rape Shield Laws

The defense usually attempts to undermine the sex crime victim's credibility by exploring the victim's sexual history and reputation. It is because of this embarrassment that the majority of sexual assaults go unreported to police. Over the last two decades, many states have passed laws to reform the procedures for prosecuting sexual assault so that permissible evidence focuses on the specific facts of the alleged assault, rather than the victim's past sexual conduct. In fact, most states have passed legislation—known as "rape shield" laws—prohibiting the introduction of the victim's past sexual history into evidence.

In addition to these state laws, the Safe Streets for Women Act, as set forth above, amended the Federal Rules of Evidence to prohibit the admission of evidence offered to prove: (i) that a victim engaged in other sexual behavior; or (ii) a victim's alleged sexual predisposition. The only exceptions to the federal rules apply in criminal cases where: (i) evidence of specific instances of sexual behavior by the victim are offered to prove that a person other than the accused was the actual perpetrator; (ii) evidence of specific instances of sexual behavior by the victim with respect to the accused are offered to prove consent; and (iii) the evidence, if excluded, would violate the defendant's constitutional rights.

In addition, in a civil case, evidence offered to prove the sexual behavior or sexual predisposition of a victim is admissible if its probative value substantially outweighs the danger of harm to any victim and unfair prejudice to any party. Nevertheless, evidence of a victim's reputation is admissible only if it has been placed in controversy by the victim.

Similar Crimes Evidence in Sex Offense Cases

The Violent Crime Control and Law Enforcement Act enacted general rules of admissibility in federal sexual assault and child molestation cases for evidence that the defendant has committed other similar offenses, facilitating the effective prosecution of habitual sex offenders. The new evidence rules provide the basis for informed decisions by juries regarding questions of propensity to commit future crimes in light of the defendant's past conduct. This amendment to the Federal Rules of Evidence has served as a model for the states, which prosecute the majority of sex offense crimes.

Confidential Communications for Rape Victims

Unfortunately, when a woman who has been victimized by sexual assault reports the crime and seeks help through counseling, she all too often finds herself victimized again when the attorney defending the sex offender issues subpoenas for her counseling records. Because many sexual assault and domestic violence counselors are not psychologists or psychotherapists, they cannot claim that such communications are privileged under many state statutes.

In order to encourage victims of sexual assault to report the crimes, the victims must be able to communicate freely and confidentially with their counselors. Without this guarantee of confidentiality, sexual assault and domestic violence victims will continue to be reluctant to report these serious crimes, and will avoid seeking necessary crisis intervention and counseling.

Establishing statutory testimonial privileges for sexual assault and domestic violence counselors will help ensure that these important communications will remain confidential and that victims will not be reluctant to report the crimes and seek help. To address this important concern, the majority of states and the District of Columbia have enacted statutes that protect these confidential communications.

Rape-Related Post-Traumatic Stress Disorder (RR-PTSD)

According to the National Victim Center, nearly one-third of all rape victims develop what is known as Rape-related Post-traumatic Stress Disorder (RR-PTSD) at some point in their life following the attack.

The first symptom of RR-PTSD is the feeling of reliving the traumatic experience. This occurs when the victim is unable to block out remembrances—e.g. flashbacks—about the rape incident. There are often accompanying nightmares in which the victim relives the whole experience. In addition, the victim often feels overwhelming distress when confronted with stimuli which symbolize the trauma.

Another major symptom of RR-PTSD is social withdrawal, also referred to as "psychogenic numbing," which leaves the victim feeling emotionally dead. The victim no longer experiences normal feelings such as those felt prior to the traumatic incident. For example, victims may no longer feel the normal range of human emotions, such as happiness and sorrow. Survivors of crime victims may also experience a decreased interest in living. The victim is also likely to develop a form of amnesia concerning the details of the experience. This is a defense mechanism which takes over to protect the victim from experiencing further psychic trauma.

A third major symptom of RR-PTSD involves avoidance behavior. Avoidance behavior occurs when the victim attempts to avoid any thoughts, feelings or contacts which might stimulate a remembrance of the trauma. For example, a rape victim may refuse to drive in the area close to where the sexual assault occurred.

The fourth set of symptoms include an exaggerated startle response, inability to sleep, memory impairment, and difficulty concentrating. Victims may also exhibit episodes of anger and irritability which have no identifiable cause. Rape victims are three times more likely to suffer major depressive episodes as compared to those who have not been victimized. In addition, rape victims are 4.1 times more likely to contemplate suicide, and thirteen percent actually follow through with a suicide attempt. Some also develop drug and alcohol problems following the traumatic experience.

Sexually Transmitted Disease

An additional factor in the psychological trauma associated with sexual assault is the fear that the victim has been exposed to a sexually transmitted disease and, in particular, to the potentially deadly and widespread HIV infection. The fear is real and greatly exacerbates the stress a victim of sexual assault is already caused to endure.

Following the assault, the victim must make the decision on whether to be tested. It is recommended that the victim receive counseling both before and after being tested for HIV infection. If they wish to be tested, it is important that the test be taken as soon after the assault as possible for a baseline reading. If the test results are negative, it is suggested that additional testing take place every six months for the following eighteen months. Of course, if the test results are positive, the impact will be devastating and intensive counseling will be required.

Nevertheless, the victim should be aware that a positive HIV test does not mean he or she has, or will develop, full-blown AIDS. Further, medical treatment has advanced to the point where death is not imminent, and some HIV infected individuals experience little, if any, symptoms.

Sexual Assault and Date Rape

Alcohol and drugs are known to be a significant factor in the sexual assault of young women by young men with whom they are acquainted. This is generally referred to as "date rape" or "acquaintance rape," and has become a problem on college campuses. According to the National College Women Sexual Victimization (NCWSV) study, 20–25 percent of college women are victims of an attempted or completed rape, and in 9 out of 10 cases, the offenders are known to the victims.

In fact, 12.8 percent of completed rapes, 35.0 percent of attempted rapes, and 22.9 percent of threatened rapes take place during a date. Although a woman's behavior does not cause acquaintance rape, it appears that frequent or excessive drinking is a contributing factor.

Sexual assault and acquaintance rape results from multiple factors, including the offender's misperception of verbal and nonverbal cues, particularly when alcohol and drugs are involved. In fact, most men who commit acquaintance rape or sexual assault are not even aware that their behavior is offensive or unreasonable. Because alcohol slows motor functions, reducing the likelihood that a woman can verbally or physically resist an attack, the perpetrator often misinterprets this lack of resistance as consent.

Date Rape Drugs

There are also a variety of drugs that are used to overpower a woman's will, or even cause her to suffer blackouts during which time a sexual assault takes place. These drugs have become known as "date rape drugs." Although alcohol is the most commonly used date rape "drug," other nonalcoholic date rape drugs include marijuana, cocaine, rohypnol, gamma hydroxybutyrate (GHB), benzodiazepines, ketamine, barbiturates, chloral hydrate, methaqualone, heroin, morphine, LSD, and other hallucinogens. Because of the serious side effects of these drugs, and their impact on memory, victims who are given the drugs oftentimes cannot recall whether they were actually sexually assaulted.

Male Rape Victims

Although this chapter is primarily focused on violence against women, it should be pointed out that male rape is prevalent and is more underreported than female sexual assault. The perpetrators of these crimes are primarily other males. In the past, the subject of male rape has not received a lot of attention, in large part due to prevailing attitudes about sex in general. Little research has been conducted on this subject, and the effects of these crimes on the victims.

Nevertheless, because studies have concluded that sexual assault is borne of aggression, and not motivated by sexual desire, this would suggest that the gender or age of the victim may in some cases be irrelevant. The research that has been undertaken concerning the psychological effects of rape on male victims demonstrates that males experience similar reactions, including depression, anger, and guilt.

Males also experience sexual dysfunction and a damaged self-image following such an attack.

Because of prevailing attitudes, males are even more reluctant to report the crime than female rape victims. It is a fact that society generally believes that men should be able to protect themselves and are more at fault for allowing a rape to take place. Thus, there is less sympathy for the male victim, who does not receive the emotional support given his female counterpart.

One of the biggest reasons males fail to report rape is their fear of being identified as a homosexual. This is so even though, as stated earlier, sexual assault is an act of aggression, power and control, and the sexual orientation of the perpetrator and/or the victim is largely irrelevant. The fact is that male rape is a violent crime that affects heterosexual men as well as homosexual men.

In fact, knowledge of the male's reluctance to report a sexual assault is so common that criminals have been known to rape their male victims merely because they know that this will deter the victim from reporting the crime. In addition, the commission of hate crimes against homosexuals ironically often includes incidents of forcible rape accompanied by verbal harassment and other forms of violent assault.

DOMESTIC VIOLENCE

Domestic violence generally refers to felony or misdemeanor crimes of violence committed by a current or former spouse of the victim, by a person with whom the victim shares a child in common; by a person who is cohabiting or has cohabited with the victim as a spouse; or by a person similarly situated to a spouse—also generally referred to as an "intimate."

Historically, domestic violence was often viewed as a private family matter, and that it was nobody's right to interfere. Law enforcement often took the position that domestic violence was not a criminal offense. The victim was all too often blamed for causing the abusive behavior—e.g. "button pushing." As a result, the victim frequently remained silent about the abuse, rather than suffer criticism and shame, and possible retaliation by the abuser for involving the police.

By enacting the Violence Against Women Act, as discussed above, the federal government demonstrated its commitment, along with states, local governmental units, and tribal governments, to put an end to the silence, to create tougher legislation, and to require greater police protection for domestic violence victims.

STATISTICS

Research demonstrates that women are more at risk for being victims of domestic violence than their male counterparts. It is estimated that 6 million women are assaulted by their husbands or male companions every year, a significant number of which are considered to involve severe injuries. According to the Federal Bureau of Investigation, in 1993, 29% of female murder victims were killed by their husbands, former husbands, or boyfriends. In this same time period, only 3% of male victims were killed by their wives, former wives, or girlfriends.

While friends and acquaintances of women victims committed more than half of the rapes and sexual assaults, intimates committed 26 percent, and strangers were responsible for about one in five. In fact, women were attacked about six times more often by offenders with whom they had an intimate relationship than were male violence victims. Men, however, were more likely than women to experience violent crimes committed by both acquaintances and strangers. In fact, men were about twice as likely as women to experience acts of violence by strangers.

PROFILE OF THE VICTIM

Women between the ages of 20 and 34 were the most likely of all ages to be victimized by an intimate. In addition, women of all races were about equally vulnerable to attacks by intimates. Nevertheless, women in families with incomes below $10,000 per year were more likely than other women to be violently attacked by an intimate.

Women living in central cities, suburban areas and rural locations experience similar rates of violence committed by intimates. Divorced or separated women had higher rates of violence by intimates than married women or women who never married. College graduates had the lower rates of violence committed by intimates compared to women with less than a high school education.

PROFILE OF THE OFFENDER

Research has indicated a number of identifying factors which place a man at risk as a potential batterer, including: (i) unemployment; (ii) poverty; (iii) drug or alcohol use; (iv) witnessing spousal abuse among parents as a child; (v) lack of education; and (vi) age 18 to 30 years old.

A recent study suggests that possessiveness is the most prevalent reason given by male offenders for killing their partners, and spousal homicide occurs more frequently during a period when the couple are separated, particularly if the separation was initiated by the wife.

Over half of the defendants convicted of killing their spouse had prior criminal records, although they were less likely to have a criminal history than defendants who had killed non-family members. In addition, as compared to non-family murder defendants, intimates were less likely to be unemployed, but more likely to have a history of mental illness.

Statistics gathered from a 1988 study of murder cases in large urban counties determined that the majority of defendants who killed their spouses were male (60%) and over the age of 30 (77%), as compared to the majority of defendants who killed non-family murders, who were overwhelmingly male (93%) and under the age of 30 (65%). Approximately 80% of the defendants in the 1988 study of spousal murder cases were convicted or plead guilty.

Characteristics of a Spousal Murder Case

According to the BJS, over one third of spousal murders took place during the day, the majority of which took place at home (86%). Most defendants murdered only their spouse. Over half of the defendants had been drinking alcohol at the time of the murder, and almost half of the victims had also been drinking at the time the offense took place.

In approximately 23% of the incidents, the murdered spouses allegedly precipitated the incident by provoking the defendant, e.g. with a deadly weapon, nonlethal weapon or other physical contact.

In addition, over 62% of the defendants accused of murdering their spouses were arrested on the day the crime took place as compared to 32% of defendants accused of killing non-family members.

Protection Orders

A domestic violence victim is often advised to obtain a protection order. A protection order is basically an injunction issued by the court for the purpose of preventing violent or threatening acts of domestic violence. A protection order in a domestic relationship is usually obtained by filing a petition with the Family Court of the jurisdiction where the victim lives. An order of protection is issued on either a temporary or permanent basis.

The court will likely issue a temporary order of protection, upon the filing of the petition, based on the victim's allegations that she is in imminent danger of physical harm. The abuser is entitled to respond to the allegations contained in the petition for a protection order. If it is determined that the allegations are true, a permanent protection order will be issued. The maximum length of time a protection order may last varies according to state law.

A typical protection order may (i) prohibit the abuser from contacting the victim; (ii) prohibit the abuser from further abusing or harassing the victim; (iii) require the abuser to provide support to the victim and children; and/or (iv) require counseling.

After a victim has obtained a protection order, she can call the police if the abuser violates it. In some states, police are required to arrest the abuser if there appears to be a violation, e.g. the abuser is found outside the victim's home.

Full Faith and Credit

The VAWA's "full faith and credit" provision requires states to honor protection orders issued by other jurisdictions. The victim does not have to register a protection order in the second state for it to be effective because the protection order of the issuing state provides continuous protection to the victim. Unfortunately, statistics have shown that no piece of paper can completely protect a domestic violence victim from an abuser who is intent on causing physical harm.

Federal Interstate Domestic Violence Enforcement

Victims of domestic violence often seek safety and shelter with friends and relatives living in other states, where they are often followed by their abusers. The VAWA addressed this problem by establishing new federal offenses in cases where an abuser crosses state lines to violate a protection order or injure, harass or intimidate a spouse or intimate partner.

These provisions are crucial to prosecuting cases where the abuser's travel across state lines makes state prosecution difficult, and/or where state penalties may not be tough enough to deter the abusive behavior. They also provide additional important benefits for domestic violence victims, including strengthened restitution provisions and the right to address the court prior to a pre-trial release of the defendant concerning the victim's concerns about danger posed by the defendant's release.

The VAWA authorizes severe federal sentences for abusers who travel interstate with the intent to injure, harass or intimidate a domestic partner or violate a protection order. The VAWA also ensures that the law follows an abuser who crosses state lines, and provides victims with protection throughout the United States.

Weapon Use

Approximately 18% of rape, robbery and assault victims faced an intimate who was armed compared to those attacked by strangers (33%), other relatives (22%), and acquaintances (21%). In 40% of the intimate victimizations, a knife or sharp instrument was the weapon of choice, guns were involved in 34% of the attacks, and 15% of the attacks involved other weapons. Guns were more likely to be used in attacks by strangers. Nevertheless, women were actually injured by intimates in 52 percent of the attacks, compared to 20 percent of the attacks by strangers.

Approximately 62% of murder victims killed by intimates in 1992 were shot to death. Guns were used to kill wives or ex-wives 69% of the time, and girlfriends in 60% of those cases. Husbands and ex-husbands were also primarily killed by guns in 61% of the homicides, whereas knives were used to murder boyfriends 54% of the time. Nevertheless, there were less murders involving guns for victims killed by intimates than for victims killed by strangers or acquaintances.

The Firearms Disability Provision

The Violent Crime Control and Law Enforcement Act includes a provision that makes it unlawful for persons subject to certain restraining orders to possess firearms. This provision is designed to protect victims of domestic violence. The firearms disability provision provides some measure of security to victims in that their abusers can be arrested if they attempt to purchase or possess firearms during the period of the restraining order.

Mandatory Arrest Policies

Police officers have historically been reluctant to become involved in domestic violence disputes, largely because such calls for police assistance are among the most complex, emotionally charged and potentially dangerous calls to which police respond. Nevertheless, many jurisdictions have implemented mandatory arrest policies.

A mandatory arrest policy requires police to arrest a domestic assault offender whenever the officer determines that a crime has been committed and probable cause for arrest exists. Currently, the majority of states and the District of Columbia have adopted mandatory arrest policies. These policies convey a message to the victim, the family, and the community that domestic violence is a serious crime that will not be tolerated.

Nevertheless, statistics show that punishment of a person convicted of domestic violence is still less severe than a perpetrator of violence against a stranger. In fact, an individual convicted of murdering their spouse generally receives a much less severe sentence than one who commits murder against non-family members. For example, one study showed that approximately 90% of spouse murderers receive an average prison sentence of only 13 years.

Rural Domestic Violence Enforcement

If a domestic violence victim in a rural area of this country needs assistance, she may be faced with many difficulties. Very few police officers patrol in small rural communities, therefore, it may be too late once a call for assistance is answered. In addition, there is understandable fear that any report of abuse will not remain a secret in small communities.

Geographic isolation, culturally close communities, and lack of domestic violence information and services are among the problems unique to rural areas. Victims in rural areas also may not trust anyone outside their communities to protect them from their abusers. Therefore, they may elect to continue living in emotional isolation rather than seek help. Because rural areas in the United States are also experiencing growth in their immigrant populations, victims may be further isolated as a result of language and cultural barriers.

In response to this problem, the VAWA has established monetary grant programs to (i) create training programs for those individuals most likely to be in contact with rural domestic violence victims, such as law enforcement, shelter workers, health care providers, and clergy; (ii) increase public awareness and implement community education campaigns; and (iii) expand direct services for rural victims.

Strategies for the Domestic Violence Victim

It is important for women who are in abusive relationships to recognize the risk factors, and to prepare themselves for the possibility of flight in case the situation becomes dangerous. The following advice and information has been gathered from nationwide domestic violence organizations, such as the National Victim Center, in order to give the domestic violence victim some coping strategies at various stages of a domestic violence relationship.

Strategies While Still in the Abusive Relationship

A victim of domestic violence is advised to immediately leave the abusive relationship to avoid serious personal injury to herself or the children. Nevertheless, it is recognized that many women, for whatever reason, try to endure the violent behavior for as long as possible. In those cases, the following advice should be heeded:

1. If it appears that abuse is about to occur, don't be combative. Try to diffuse the situation by backing down or leaving the situation to allow your partner to cool off.

2. Prepare safety areas in your home where you can go if you must escape abuse. Keep all types of weapons, if any, locked up in a remote

location. If an abusive situation appears imminent, go to the safety area.

3. Maintain a phone in that area in case you need to call for help. Try to remember a list of important phone numbers, such as the police, ambulance, shelter, and hotline numbers, including the national domestic violence hotline number which is further discussed below.

4. If you have children, try to stay away from them during an abusive episode so that they do not also become targets of the abuser.

5. If you are unable to avoid the violent attack, protect vulnerable areas of your body,—e.g. your head and face—by blocking with your arms.

6. Don't hide your situation from family and close friends. You may have to rely on them for help if the situation gets really out of hand.

7. Teach your children how to get help if the need arises. Caution them not to involve themselves in the altercation. Explain to them that violence is wrong, and they are not at fault.

Making Plans to Leave the Abusive Relationship

If the relationship becomes too turbulent and unpredictable to endure, the domestic violence victim must make plans to leave the situation. In that case, the following advice should be heeded.

1. Maintain a journal of all of the violent incidents, and keep it and any evidence of physical abuse, such as photographs, in a safe place where you will have access to them after you leave.

2. If you are injured, seek medical care at the emergency room of a hospital or your physician. Make sure your account of the injuries is documented.

3. Contact your local battered women's shelter for information about your legal rights, sources of financial assistance, counseling and other available resources. Again, the national domestic violence hotline is also equipped to provide resource information to victims.

4. If you are unemployed, seek out job training and educational programs to help prepare you for entering the workforce.

5. Practice an escape plan in case the need arises. Plan for all possible contingencies. For example, get into the habit of having your car ready for emergency departures and a spare set of keys in case yours are confiscated. Hide some emergency money, and keep a suitcase packed with some essential clothing and supplies for yourself and your children.

Leaving the Abusive Relationship

Once you decide to leave:

1. Ask the police to accompany you while you remove your personal belongings from the home and to escort you from the home.

2. Make sure you take with you important items that you will need and may not want to risk reentering the home to retrieve, such as your drivers license; legal documents, such as your marriage license, birth certificates, citizenship documents and social security cards; banking information and checkbook; property ownership documents, such as titles and deeds; credit cards; medical records and prescription medication; school records; insurance information; personal valuables and effects; and your personal telephone book with important phone numbers.

3. Try to create a false trail so that the abuser cannot easily track you down. Don't use calling card numbers that can be traced back to your whereabouts. Don't use credit cards in areas that you intend to relocate.

After you successfully leave the violent relationship, seek advice from domestic violence organizations on how to proceed to protect yourself and your children from further abuse. Court intervention may be necessary. In extreme cases, relocation may be the only alternative.

A directory of state domestic violence coalitions is set forth at Appendix 19; and a directory of national domestic violence organizations is set forth at Appendix 20.

THE NATIONAL DOMESTIC VIOLENCE HOTLINE

In 1996, as authorized by the VAWA, a nationwide, 24-hour toll-free domestic violence hotline was implemented. The hotline is the first federally funded national domestic violence hotline in this country. The hotline provides help for domestic violence victims across the country 24-hours a day, 365 days a year. The service is toll-free, operating throughout the United States, Puerto Rico, and the Virgin Islands.

The hotline is designed to help create a more seamless system among local, state, and national service providers. Although there are already a number of local domestic violence hotlines in place, many areas in this country still lack a comprehensive response system. The national hotline is especially important for victims who live in rural or isolated areas which may lack their own local hotlines or other comprehensive domestic violence services.

When someone calls the hotline, they speak to a trained domestic violence advocate, who offers them crisis intervention, support, and referrals to local services in their community. The advocate has access to a national database that contains the most current information on emergency shelters, legal advocacy, social services, and other programs in communities across the country. In an emergency, the hotline is also equipped to connect callers to their local police. Services are also available to the hearing impaired, and translators are available for non-English speaking victims of domestic violence.

The National Domestic Violence Hotline can be reached at 1-800-799-SAFE. The TDD number for the hearing impaired is 1-800-787-3224. It is important to note that callers who need help in an emergency should always call "911" directly for immediate assistance.

A resource directory for victims of domestic violence is set forth at Appendix 21.

CHAPTER 6:
STALKING

IN GENERAL

The term "stalking" describes any unwanted contact by an individual—referred to as a "stalker"—and his or her victim, which places the victim in fear for his or her safety. The act of stalking is not new. It is essentially conduct which was previously described as a form of harassment. Only recently has stalking been categorized as a separate offense, in large part due to the number of celebrity victims who have been subjected to stalking.

Stalking behaviors may include following the victim, making harassing phone calls, leaving notes, showing up at the victim's place of business, and vandalizing the victim's property. The stalker's actions may or may not culminate in violent behavior. As set forth below, the legal definition of stalking varies according to state law, which may specifically define prohibited stalking behavior.

STALKING STATISTICS

According to a 1998 study by the National Institute of Justice, it is estimated that approximately one million women and 400,000 men are stalked each year in the United States. Of those surveyed, eight percent of women and two percent of men said they had been stalked at some point in their lives. This would translate into 8.2 million female and two million male lifetime stalking victims. While the crime of stalking is gender neutral, 78 percent of the stalking victims identified by the study were women, and 22 percent were men.

According to the study, approximately half of all female stalking victims reported their victimization to police, and about 25 percent obtained an order of protection. However, eighty percent of all restraining orders obtained resulted in a violation by the stalker. The reported cases resulted in prosecution about 24% of the time for female victims, and about 19% for male victims. Fifty-four percent of those prosecutions resulted in convictions, and approximately 63% of convictions resulted in confinement.

Approximately 30% of stalking episodes involved vandalism of the victim's property. The majority of stalking episodes involved spying on the victim, whereas in 45% of the cases, the stalker made overt threats to the victim. Episodes of stalking generally lasted one year or less, although there are reported cases of stalking continuing for five or more years.

PROFILE OF A STALKING VICTIM

A stalking victim can be either male or female, however, most victims are female. Most stalking victims are acquainted with their stalker, who is generally alone. This is particularly so in the case of women, who are most often stalked by a current or former spouse, or a boyfriend. Studies indicate that the stalking behavior in such cases often ceases when the stalker begins a relationship with a new mate.

Men are more likely to be stalked by a stranger, and half of the time, the stalkers have an accomplice. Young adults are most often the victims of stalking. In fact, more than one-half of all stalking victims are age 18 to 29.

PROFILE OF A STALKER

Although most stalkers are male (87%), a stalker can be any gender. Stalkers come from all types of backgrounds. Because this phenomenon has only recently been subjected to scientific study, clear psychological profiles have not yet been determined. However, forensic psychologists generally place stalkers in one of three broad categories: (i) Love Obsession Stalkers; (ii) Simple Obsession Stalkers; and (iii) Erotomanic Stalkers.

Love Obsession Stalkers

A love obsession stalker is one who becomes fixated on an individual with whom they have no relationship, e.g. a total stranger or someone who they barely know. Love obsession stalkers account for approximately one-fourth of all stalking behavior.

Psychologists believe that most love obsession stalkers suffer from schizophrenia or paranoia which is manifested in delusional thoughts and behavior. Their inability to function normally in relationships causes them to create a fantasy life in which their victim plays an important role as their love interest. They then proceed to try and live out this fantasy life.

Of course, the victims are unaware of their role in this obsession, and are unwilling to participate. In turn, this causes the stalker concern as he or she tries to make the victim conform to his or her role. The stalker may resort to threats, intimidation, and even violence, so that their fantasy can be brought to fruition.

Simple Obsession Stalkers

A simple obsession stalker is one who is obsessed with an individual with whom they had a previous personal relationship. This category makes up the majority of stalking behavior. The simple obsession stalker is commonly an ex-husband or mate who desires to control his former partner. "Fatal attraction" stalkers—individuals who become obsessed during a casual short-term relationship—also fall under this category.

Simple obsession stalkers generally do not have a mental disorder as do love obsession stalkers; however, psychologists do believe these individuals suffer serious personality disorders, similar to those exhibited by physical abusers in domestic violence situations.

The characteristics which appear to be common to all simple obsession stalkers, include: (i) the inability to maintain relationships; (ii) extreme jealousy and possessiveness; (iii) emotional immaturity and insecurity; (iv) low self-esteem; and (v) the need to control their partners through intimidation and/or violence.

Thus, once their partner leaves, this rejection causes their self-esteem to plummet as they become paranoid about their loss of control over that person. They become obsessed with regaining possession and total control over their former mate. If they are unable to do so, they often resort to violence—e.g., "if I can't have him/her, nobody else will." In fact, there is a very high incidence of spousal murder associated with domestic violence victims who decide to leave their partners.

Nevertheless, the behavior of stalkers is often unpredictable. That is what makes the crime so dangerous. The perpetrator may be sending love letters and roses one day, and the following day physically assault the object of their obsession. Conversely, the stalker may engage in non-threatening stalking behavior for many, many months without ever escalating to a more aggressive stage.

Erotomanic Stalkers

Similar to love obsession stalkers, the erotomanic stalker is usually a female who suffers from a delusional belief that they are passionately loved by another. They go to great lengths to contact the person of their delusion, usually a person of higher socio-economic class and status, or an unattainable public figure. These stalkers are often described as celebrity stalkers or obsessed fans.

LEGISLATION

In 1990, California became the first state to pass a law which specifically defined stalking as a crime. This action was taken in response to several cases in which stalking victims were eventually murdered. These victims had previously tried to make complaints to the police about the stalking behavior, however, the existing law required that the offender take some affirmative action before they could make an arrest. This requirement was changed with the new stalking law, permitting police to intervene at an earlier stage. A 1999 amendment to the law added prohibitions on the use of the internet and other electronic means for stalking.

The text of the California anti-stalking statute is set forth at Appendix 22.

State Anti-stalking Laws

After California enacted its anti-stalking statute, all 50 states followed by enacting some type of anti-stalking legislation. Although the specific provisions may vary state by state, they all generally prohibit stalking behaviors that are intimidating and place the victim in fear for his or her safety. Most states statutes define stalking as the willful, malicious, and repeated following and harassing of another person. Some of the statutes identify specific acts of stalking, such as surveillance, telephone harassment, vandalism, and specify how many acts of stalking must occur in order to qualify as stalking. Many statutes also require that the alleged stalker must make a credible threat of violence against the victim to be actionable whereas some statutes deem the stalking conduct itself as the credible threat.

The reader is advised to check the law of his or her own jurisdiction for specific provisions of their state stalking law.

National Institute of Justice Model Anti-stalking Statute

In addition to the state statutes, the National Institute of Justice has promulgated a model anti-stalking statute. The statute defines stalking as a course of conduct directed at a specific person that involves repeated visual or physical proximity, nonconsensual communication, or verbal, written or implied threats, or a combination thereof, that would cause a reasonable person fear. The statute requires victims to experience a high level of fear of bodily harm as a result of the stalking behavior, but does not require that the stalker make a credible threat of violence against the victim.

The statute encourages legislators to: (i) make stalking a felony offense; (ii) establish penalties for stalking that are commensurate with the seriousness of the crime; (iii) provide criminal justice officials with the authority to arrest, prosecute, and sentence stalkers.

The Violence Against Women Act—Subtitle F

Further, a federal law prohibits an individual from crossing state lines for the purposes of stalking his or her victim. The National Stalker and Domestic Violence Reduction Section, (Subtitle F) of the Violence Against Women Act (VAWA), addresses the problem of stalking. The law authorizes access to information from national crime information databases consisting of identification records, criminal history records, protection orders and wanted person records by civil or criminal courts in connection with stalking or domestic violence cases.

In addition, this section authorizes federal and state criminal justice agencies to enter information into the criminal information database concerning individuals who have been arrested or convicted on stalking charges, or for whom arrest warrants or protection orders for stalking are pending.

The law also provides monetary grants to states and local governmental units to establish programs and improve procedures for entering data regarding stalking and domestic violence incidents into local, state and national crime information databases.

The Interstate Anti-Stalking Punishment and Prevention Act

The Interstate Anti-Stalking Punishment and Prevention Act was enacted by Congress in 1996 in order to improve existing anti-stalking provisions and create a uniform federal law to protect stalking victims when they travel across state lines. Anyone who travels across state lines with the intent to injure or harass another person, and in the course of such travel, places that person in reasonable fear of death or serious bodily injury to that person or a member of his or her immediate family, would be in violation of federal law. The Act also applies to stalking behavior which take place on all federal property, including military installations, and when entering or exiting Indian territory. A violation of the statute is a felony.

SAFETY STRATEGIES AND TIPS

When dealing with a former mate who is engaged in stalking conduct, one must advise the stalker, in a firm and direct manner, that they do no wish to be contacted. Avoid any language that sounds unsure, that the stalker may misinterpret as the possibility of another chance. Under no circumstances should the victim contact the stalker.

A stalking victim who is being subjected to particularly threatening behavior should go to the nearest police station and immediately report the crime. If it is not possible to find a nearby police station at the time, safety may be sought at a church, shelter or other public place where a stalker is less likely to make a scene. Until the situation is brought under control, the stalking victim may consider relocating to a location where he or she will not be found.

If the danger is not imminent, but the potential for violence is there, a stalking victim should consider petitioning the court for an order of protection, as discussed in Chapter 5 of this almanac. Again, however, the reader is cautioned that an order of protection is merely a piece of paper, and will not stop a perpetrator who is intent on harming his or her victim.

In the meantime, one must make sure that their personal information is kept private, including their address, telephone number, and social security number. The stalking victim should have an unpublished and unlisted telephone number, and should change their e-mail address if they are being harassed on the internet. In addition, one should order call blocking so that their telephone number is not reflected on the caller ID of the person who placed the call.

INTERNET STALKING

As the worldwide web developed and became more accessible to the average citizen, stalkers found a new medium through which to harass their victims. Law enforcement agencies estimate that electronic communications are a factor in 20 percent to 40 percent of all stalking cases.

Internet stalking, also known as cyberstalking, is popular with stalkers because of the relative anonymity of the system. Many stalkers who have been deterred from physically stalking their victim due to a restraining order or threatened criminal prosecution, turn to the internet to carry on their behaviors. Threatening and harassing emails can be sent to victims from virtually any computer with internet access.

Forty-five states now have laws that explicitly include electronic forms of communication within stalking or harassment laws. State laws that do not include specific references to electronic communication may still apply to those who threaten or harass others through the internet.

A table of state anti-cyberstalking and harassment laws is set forth at Appendix 23.

PROSECUTION

Although stalking laws no longer require the victim to wait until the stalker takes some affirmative action, the victim is still required to provide sufficient evidence to establish probable cause that the perpetrator engaged in illegal conduct. The victim is advised to keep a journal documenting each stalking incident. Photographs and videotapes, voice mail messages, correspondence and witness affidavits are types of evidence that may be used to establish probable cause. The victim should also obtain a copy of their state stalking statute to find out what behavior constitutes a stalking offense so that the proof obtained will convince law enforcement that a violation has taken place.

The evidence should be taken to the appropriate law enforcement official. If they refuse to investigate the conduct, the victim should take their case to the local district attorney's office and speak with a prosecutor.

CHAPTER 7:
SCHOOL VIOLENCE

IN GENERAL

Disruptive—and often criminal—behavior is a serious problem in the nation's schools, particularly in large urban schools. Although much of the criminal behavior is nonviolent, such as vandalism and theft, there are an alarming number of violent offenses committed against students, as well as teachers, often involving weapons.

Sadly, schools are no longer a safe haven where children are sent to learn and mature. In fact, many schools have become armed camps where children are no longer greeted at the door by their teachers, but are confronted by dogs who are trained to sniff them for drugs, and metal detectors designed to expose illegal weapons. The nature of the violence is even more alarming. School officials are not just breaking up fistfights any more. They are confiscating drugs and weapons, dodging bullets, and rushing critically injured children to emergency rooms.

Unfortunately, violence has become an expected part of the day in many schools. Robberies, shootings, and other physical attacks are common, particularly in large urban areas. Children are afraid to go to school for fear that they will be killed, in large part due to the accessibility of guns to young people. Otherwise peaceful students have resorted to carrying illegal handguns for the sole purpose of self-defense. As set forth below, the statistics concerning school violence continue to be a major concern.

SCHOOL VIOLENCE STATISTICS

Violence at School or on School Property

Although school violence continues to be a serious problem for the nation's schools, statistics compiled by the Bureau of Justice Statistics

(BJS) indicates that, in general, crime in schools is on the decline. Violent victimization rates for students varied from a high of 59 violent victimizations per 1,000 students in 1993 to a low of 26 per 1,000 students in 2000. In addition, the percentage of students who said they were victims of crime at school, both violent and property crimes, decreased from 10% of all students in 1995 to 6% in 2001.

Despite this decline, the numbers are still alarming. In 1993, 1995, 1997, 1999, and 2001, between 7 and 9 percent of students reported being threatened or injured in the previous 12 months with a weapon such as a gun, knife, or club on school property.

From July 1998 to June 1999, there were 47 school-associated violent deaths. Thirty-eight of these violent deaths were homicides; six were suicides; a law enforcement officer in the line of duty killed two students; and one death was unintentional.

According to the BJS, there was no reliable indication of either an increase or decrease in violent school-associated deaths during their 7-year study. From July 1992 through June 1999, there were 358 school-associated violent deaths, including 255 deaths of children age 5 to 19. Of this total, 218 were homicides of school-aged children and 37 were suicides of school-aged children.

According to the National Crime Victimization Survey (NCVS), from 1993 to 2001, about 703,800 violent crimes against persons age 12 to 17 occurred annually at school or on school property. About 8% of these crimes were committed with a weapon, of which about 1% were committed with a firearm. About one-third of armed assaults in schools resulted in injury to the victim.

In addition, approximately 172 homicides of both students and nonstudents took place at school or on school property. Of these, 18% were committed with a knife or other sharp object, and 69% were committed with a firearm. Of the firearm homicides at school, three-quarters were committed with handguns.

The percentage of students in grades 9 through 12 who have been threatened or injured with a weapon on school property has not changed significantly in recent years. In 1993, 1995, and 1997, about 7 to 8 percent of students reported being threatened or injured with a weapon such as a gun, knife, or club on school property in the prior 12 months.

Violence Away from School Compared to Violence in School

Studies show that students are more likely to be victims of serious violent crime away from school than at school. According to the BJS study, in each year surveyed from 1993 through 2000, school-aged children were at least 70 times more likely to be murdered away from school than they were to be murdered at school. In fact, during this time frame, there were 2,358 homicides of children age 5 to 19 away from school, and 1,855 suicides in the same age group.

From July 1, 1997 through June 30, 1998, a total of 2,752 children age 5 to 19 were victims of homicide in the United States. During this same time period, students age 12 to 18 were more likely to be victims of nonfatal serious violent crime—including rape, sexual assault, robbery, and aggravated assault—away from school than when they were at school.

In 1998, approximately 550,000 students in this age range were victims of these crimes away from schools, compared with about 253,000 at school. In addition, students in this age range were also victims of about 1.2 million nonfatal violent crimes at school compared to about 1.3 million away from school.

As for non-violent crimes, such as theft, students age 12 to 18 were more likely to be victims at school than away from school in 1998. Approximately 1.6 million thefts occurred at school compared to about 1.2 million away from school.

According to the BJS study, from July 1992 through June 1999, there were 358 school-associated violent deaths of children age 5 to 9, compared to a total of 22,323 homicides and 14, 813 suicides in the same age group, which occurred away from school.

Weapon Use

According to the Bureau of Justice Statistics, in 2001, 6 percent of students in grades 9 through 12 reported carrying a weapon such as a gun, knife, or club, on school property. This represented a decline from 12 percent in 1993. Male students were at least three times more likely than females to carry a weapon on school property. For example, in 2001, 10 percent of males carried a weapon on school property, compared with 3 percent of females. In addition, few differences could be detected by race/ethnicity in the percentages of students on school property.

DEMOGRAPHICS

A 1998 study indicated that students age 12 to 18, living in urban, suburban, and rural locales were equally vulnerable to serious violent crime and theft at school. Away from school, urban and suburban students were more vulnerable to serious violent crime and theft than were rural students.

Younger students age 12 to 14 were more likely than older students age 15 to 18 to be victims of crime at school. Males were more likely than females to report being threatened or injured with a weapon on school property.

In 1999, public school students were more likely to report having been victims of violent crime during the previous 6 months than were private school students. However, public school students were equally likely as private school students to experience theft.

In 1996-1997, elementary schools were much less likely than either middle or high schools to report any type of crime, and were much more likely to report vandalism than any other crime. At the middle and high school levels, physical attack or fight without a weapon was generally the most commonly reported crime in 1996-97. Theft or larceny was more common at the high school than at the middle school level.

BULLYING

In recent years, schools have begun to introduce anti-bullying programs to students in an effort to curb school violence. Experts have determined that bullying can contribute to a climate of fear and intimidation in schools.

In 2001, students age 12 to 18 were asked if they had been bullied at school. Eight percent of students reported that they had been bullied at school in the previous 6 months, an increase from 5 percent in 1999.

In addition, both males and females were more likely to be bullied in 2001 than in 1999.

Further, the percentage of students who reported that they had been bullied increased between 1999 and 2001 for each racial/ethnic group except black students. About 6 percent of black students in both years reported they had been bullied. For white students, the percentage of students bullied increased from 5 percent to 9 percent; from 4 percent to 8 percent for Hispanic students; and from 3 percent to 7 percent for other non-Hispanic students.

In 2001, students in lower grades were generally more likely to be bullied than students in higher grades. For example, 14 percent of students in 6th grade reported being bullied, compared with 2 percent of students in grade 12.

VIOLENCE AGAINST TEACHERS

Although most violence occurs among students, teachers have also been the target of violence in the school. Unfortunately, this increase in the frequency and nature of violence against teachers has caused many excellent teachers to leave the profession for fear of their safety. The statistics are alarming.

According to the Bureau of Justice Statistics, over the 5-year period from 1996 through 2000, teachers were the victims of approximately 1,603,000 nonfatal crimes at school, including 1,004,000 thefts and 599,000 violent crimes, including rape or sexual assault, robbery, aggravated assault, and simple assault. On average, this translates into 321,000 nonfatal crimes per year, or 74 crimes per 1,000 teachers per year.

Among the violent crimes against teachers during this 5-year period, there were about 69,000 serious violent crimes, including rape or sexual assault, robbery, and aggravated assault. On average, this translates into 14,000 serious violent crimes per year.

Male teachers were more likely to be victims of violent crimes than female teachers. In addition, senior high school and middle/junior high school teachers were more likely to be victims of violent crimes than elementary school teachers.

Location played a large factor in the victimization of teachers. For example, over the 5-year period from 1996 through 2000, urban teachers were more likely to be victims of violent crimes than suburban and rural teachers. During the 1999-2000 school year, teachers in central city schools were more likely to be threatened with injury or physically attacked than were teachers in urban fringe or rural schools. In addition, public school teachers were more likely than private school teachers to be victimized by students in school.

During the 1999-2000 school year, statistics indicate that black teachers were more likely to be threatened than white teachers; however, the prevalence of teachers being attacked by students did not vary according to the racial/ethnic backgrounds of teachers.

Although criminal prosecution is carried out against perpetrators of physical violence—students and parents—the Supreme Court cited the First Amendment in striking down an attempt by several states to criminalize verbal abuse against a teacher on school premises.

PREVENTION STRATEGIES

Zero Tolerance Policies

According to the National Center for Education Statistics (NCES), three-quarters or more of all schools reported having zero tolerance policies for various student offenses. About 90 percent of schools reported zero tolerance policies for firearms (94 percent) and weapons other than firearms (91 percent). Eighty-seven and 88 percent had policies of zero tolerance for alcohol and drugs, respectively. Seventy-nine percent had a zero tolerance policy for violence. Schools with no crime reported were less likely to have a zero tolerance policy for violence (74 percent) than schools that had reported one or more serious crimes (85 percent).

Security Guards and Metal Detectors

Many schools have had to hire additional security personnel, and install safety devices, such as weapon detectors, in an effort to protect innocent students and teachers. Many states permit school officials to install metal detectors to prevent students from bringing weapons into the school. The courts have generally held that metal detectors are legal, provided they are not used in a discriminatory manner, e.g. only requiring male or minority students to pass through the metal detectors.

THE SAFE AND DRUG-FREE SCHOOLS AND COMMUNITIES ACT OF 1994

The seventh goal of the Goals 2000: Educate America Act calls for safe, disciplined, and drug-free schools. This goal was codified in the 1994 Safe and Drug-Free Schools and Communities Act of 1994 (Title IV of the Improving America's Schools Act of 1994, P.L. 103-382). This law was passed by Congress in response to reports of numerous thefts and violent crimes occurring on or near school campuses each year. The purpose of the Act is to assist the nation's schools in providing a disciplined environment which is conducive to learning by eliminating violence in and around schools and preventing illegal drug use.

The Safe and Drug-Free Schools Program is administered by the Office for Elementary and Secondary Education in the U.S. Department of Education. To achieve the goals of the Act, this program grants funds to all states each year for developing and implementing effective and research-based programs at the State and local levels that: (1) educate communities about violence and drug use; and (2) lead to fewer violent or drug-related incidents in or near schools.

CHAPTER 8:
WORKPLACE VIOLENCE

IN GENERAL

Violence plays a big role in occupational injury and death. The term workplace violence refers to violence or the threat of violence against workers. It ranges from threats and verbal abuse to physical assaults and homicide. Each week in the United States, an average of 20 workers are murdered. Approximately 18,000 workers are assaulted weekly at work. Some studies indicate that approximately 2 million American workers are victims of some type of workplace violence each year.

The National Crime Victimization Survey (NCVS) conducted a survey on workplace violence occurring between 1993 and 1999 in the United States. According to the NCVS, an average of 1.7 million violent victimizations per year were committed against persons age 12 or older who were at work or on duty. In addition to nonfatal violence, approximately 900 work-related homicides occurred annually. Workplace violence accounted for 18% of all violent crime during the 7-year period.

VULNERABLE OCCUPATIONS

Workplace violence can occur at or outside the workplace, in any workplace environment. Some industries, however, are at an increased risk for workplace violence. For example, the retail and service industries account for more than half of workplace homicides, and 85% of nonfatal workplace assaults.

Certain types of work also increase a worker's risk. This would include people who: (i) exchange money with the public; (ii) deliver passengers, goods, or services; (iii) work alone or in small groups; (iv) work during late night or early morning hours, particularly in high-crime areas; (v) work in community settings and homes where they have extensive contact with the public; (vi) guard valuables or property; and (vii) deal with violent people or volatile situations.

These workers include healthcare and social service workers such as visiting nurses, psychiatric evaluators, and probation officers; community workers such as gas and water utility employees, telephone and cable TV installers, and mail carriers; retail workers; and taxi drivers. In fact, taxi drivers have the highest risk of workplace homicides of any occupational group. According to the NCVS, police officers experienced workplace violence at rates higher than all other occupations, accounting for 261 victims per 1,000 persons.

According to the Bureau of Justice Statistics, 61% of workplace victimizations occur in private companies; 30% among government employees; and 8% of victims are self-employed. Insofar as government workers make up only 18% of the workforce, it appears that they suffer a disproportionate share of workplace attacks. This may be attributed to the fact that government jobs often involve dealing with the public and delivery of services. In addition, all local, State, and Federal police are included in this category.

A table setting forth the average annual rate of violent victimization in the workplace, by occupation of victim, from 1993 to 1999, is set forth at Appendix 24.

PERPETRATORS OF WORKPLACE VIOLENCE

In addition to robbery-related violence, perpetrators of workplace violence include customers, clients, patients, inmates, coworkers, employees or employers. The Bureau of Justice Statistics analyzed the relationship of the victim to the offender and found that female workers appeared most likely to be attacked by someone they knew, although only 5% of victimizations were attributed to an intimate, defined as a husband, ex-husband, boyfriend, or ex-boyfriend. More often, the incidents were perpetrated by a customer, client, or patient with whom the victim had an ongoing professional relationship.

A table setting forth the demographic characteristics of offenders committing workplace violence, from 1993 to 1999, is set forth at Appendix 25.

VICTIM CHARACTERISTICS

Gender

The majority of workplace homicides during 1980–92 occurred among male workers, accounting for 80% of all such homicides. The leading cause of occupational injury death varied by sex, with homicides accounting for 11% of all occupational injury deaths among male workers and 42% among female workers. Although homicide is the leading cause of occupational injury death among female workers, male workers have more than three times the risk of work-related homicide.

Race

The rate of workplace violence for white workers was 25% percent higher than blacks, and 59% higher than the rate for other races. This is a distinct difference from overall violent crime, for which blacks have the highest rates. In addition, most workplace victimizations were intraracial. About 6 in 10 white and black victims of workplace crime perceived their assailant to be of the same race.

Age

According to one study, the age of workplace homicide victims ranged from 16 to 93 during the period from 1980 to 1992. The largest number of workplace homicides occurred among workers aged 25 to 34, whereas the rate of workplace homicide increased with age. In fact, the highest rates of workplace homicide occurred among workers aged 65 and older—more than twice the rate for workers aged 55–64. These statistics applied equally to both male and female workers.

A table setting forth the average annual rate of workplace victimization by demographic characteristics of victims, from 1993 to 1999, is set forth at Appendix 26.

HOMICIDE

The most extreme form of workplace violence is homicide. Homicide is the third-leading cause of fatal occupational injury in the United States. According to the Bureau of Labor Statistics (BLS), 73% to 82% of workplace homicides occurred during a robbery or other crime, whereas only 9% to 10% were attributed to business disputes, and only 4% to 6% were attributed specifically to coworkers or former employees.

In 2001, BLS statistics indicate that there were 639 workplace homicides out of a total of 8,786 fatal workplace injuries. A total of 2,886 work-related fatalities resulted from the September 11, 2001 terrorist attack on the World Trade Center in New York. Excluding the September 11th fatalities, the overall workplace fatality count for 2001 was 5,900.

In addition, statistics indicate that the majority of workplace homicides occur in urban areas. In 1993, nearly half of all workplace homicides occurred in eight of the largest metropolitan areas. From 1993 to 1999, however, the number of workplace homicides declined 39%.

Weapon Use

According to one study, between 1980 and 1992, 76% of work-related homicides were committed with firearms, and another 12% resulted from wounds inflicted by cutting or piercing instruments. During this period, the number of firearm-related homicides declined, but then gradually increased, with the number of firearm-related workplace homicides rising to 84% in 1991.

NONFATAL ASSAULTS

According to the NCVS, from 1987 to 1992, nearly 1 million persons were assaulted annually while at work or on duty. This figure represents 15% of the total acts of violence experienced by Americans each year. Unlike homicides, statistics indicate that nonfatal workplace assaults are distributed almost equally between men and women. The majority of nonfatal assaults reported occur in the service and retail trade industries. Of those in the service industry, the majority of assaults occur in nursing homes, followed by social services and hospitals.

Nearly half of the workplace assaults are described as incidents involving hitting, kicking, or beating. There are also reported incidents of squeezing, pinching, scratching, biting, stabbing, and shooting, as well as rapes and threats of violence. Sixteen percent of workplace assaults resulted in significant injuries.

A table setting forth the average annual number, rate and percent of workplace victimization, by type of crime, from 1993 to 1999, is set forth at Appendix 27.

FAILURE TO REPORT WORKPLACE VIOLENCE

According to the NCVS, 56% of victims did not report the incident to the police. The primary reason given was that the victim believed that the incident was a minor or private matter. Approximately one-third of those surveyed stated that they did not report the incident to the police because a report had already been made to a company official.

CONSEQUENCES OF WORKPLACE VIOLENCE

According to the NCVS, workplace violence results in a significant amount of employee absences and financial costs. For example, approximately half a million workers lost 1.75 million days of work annually, and more than $55 million in wages, not including days covered by sick or annual leave, as a result of workplace violence.

Another consequence of workplace violence is the stress it produces in the workplace. There is also a catch-22 with this problem. High levels of stress may lead to violence in the workplace, but a violent incident in the workplace will most certainly lead to stress, and may even result in post-traumatic stress disorder. The employer should be sensitive to this phenomenon and provide referrals to employee assistance programs or other local mental health services for stress debriefing sessions after critical incidents of workplace violence have occurred.

PREVENTION STRATEGIES

The best protection an employer can devise in order to deter workplace violence is to establish a zero-tolerance policy. The employer should establish a workplace violence prevention program, and ensure that all employees know the policy and understand that all claims of workplace violence will be investigated and remedied promptly.

An effective workplace violence prevention program should include a system for documenting incidents, procedures to be taken in the event of incidents, and open communication between employers and workers. In addition, procedures for obtaining medical care and psychological support following violent incidents should also be addressed.

Depending on the nature of the workplace, specific methods of protection may include:

1. Safety education programs for employees so they know what conduct is not acceptable, what to do if they witness or are subjected to workplace violence, and how to protect themselves.

2. Enhanced workplace security, e.g., video surveillance, extra lighting, alarm systems; identification badges; electronic keys; and security guards.

3. Drop safes to limit the amount of cash on hand, particularly during evenings and late-night hours.

4. Cellular phones for field staff and hand-held alarms or noise devices.

5. Instructing employees not to enter any location where they feel unsafe.

6. Physical separation of workers from customers, clients, and the general public through the use of bullet-resistant barriers or enclosures in retail settings, hospital emergency departments, and social service agency claims areas, if feasible.

7. Personal protective equipment for public safety personnel, such as bulletproof vests for police officers.

8. An increase in the number of staff on duty, including the use of security guards or receptionists to screen persons entering the workplace and controlling access to actual work areas.

Although there is nothing an employee can do to prevent becoming a victim of workplace violence, there are steps a worker can take to lower their chances of becoming a victim, including learning how to recognize, avoid, or diffuse potentially violent situations by attending personal safety training programs; alerting supervisors to any concerns about safety or security; and reporting all incidents immediately in writing.

CHAPTER 9:
HATE CRIMES

IN GENERAL

Hate crimes—i.e, violence motivated by a prejudice against an individual's race, ethnicity, religion, gender or sexual orientation—are a serious threat to our society. Individuals who commit hate crimes harbor animosity and negative views towards one or more groups of people who share common characteristics.

We are not born hating certain groups of people. Such hatred is usually perpetuated by an individual's upbringing and social contacts, and rooted in ignorance. Most prejudiced individuals have no true knowledge about the people they dislike. They are influenced by other sources, including the biased portrayal of certain groups by the media, e.g. television programs and movies. They are often isolated from these groups and rely on such portrayals, along with their social conditioning, to form their own incorrect beliefs about certain groups of people, as a whole.

Most hate crimes involve assault and battery, harassment and/or vandalism, and can be particularly violent. These acts are akin to terrorism, because they are designed to create fear in the victims. Proponents of hate crimes are also known to engage in hate speech. Hate speech refers to the venemous and inciteful language one would expect to hear from such adversarial groups as the Ku Klux Klan or Neo-Nazi type groups.

Advocates for free speech argue that the First Amendment protects all speech, regardless of whether it is offensive. Nevertheless, freedom of speech does not permit conduct which intimidates, harasses or threatens another, even if that conduct is carried out through the use of words. For example, obscene telephone calls would not be protected speech.

The Supreme Court has held that non-verbal symbols of expression—which would include symbols of hate such as swastikas or burning crosses—are constitutionally protected because they are "closely akin to pure speech." Nevertheless, the First Amendment does not protect the use of non-verbal symbols used to damage or desecrate private property.

STATISTICS

According to some studies, a hate crime is committed in America every 14 minutes. In addition, this figure does not take into account the vast number of bias-related incidents that go unreported. Victims of hate crimes are often reluctant to come forward for fear that they will be re-victimized by the criminal justice system.

According to FBI statistics, the majority of hate crimes are committed against Blacks, followed by hate crimes against Whites, Jews, and homosexuals. In addition, the acts of violence were broken down into the following categories: (i) Intimidation; (ii) Simple Assault; (iii) Aggravated Assault; (iv) Murder; and (v) Forcible Rape.

LEGISLATION

Because of the unique harms caused by bias-related violence, special legislation has been enacted in many states. The reason that hate crimes needed special legislation is the recognition that the state has a compelling interest in protecting society from violence motivated by prejudice. Such violence, although largely committed against individuals, is in reality committed against society as a whole.

Hate crimes cause Americans to become suspicious and fearful of their neighbors, and creates tension in communities. Hate crimes often spawn more violence, and may lead to retaliation, resulting in a continuous vicious cycle that must be broken. Thus, to protect the peace and order of the country, it is necessary to swiftly and harshly address bias-related violence so that a clear message is sent that such behavior will not be tolerated in a just society.

Anti-bias legislation is opposed by some groups on constitutional grounds, expressing concerns over freedom of speech. In response, the U.S. Supreme Court has recently ruled that although "hate speech" cannot be banned, states have the right to punish conduct motivated by such hate.

Hate crime legislation is critical in the effort to demonstrate society's intolerance of bias-related violence. Further, hate crime legislation protects the right of an individual to be free from this type of random, senseless violence, and deters bias-related crime by severely punishing such behavior.

Currently, there are both federal and state laws which prohibit hate crimes. Many of these laws define the type of incident which qualifies as a "hate crime" and assess a greater penalty when the behavior is motivated by prejudice. For example, such laws might differentiate between a simple assault as opposed to an assault which is motivated by racial hatred, the latter receiving a harsher punishment.

Hate crime legislation generally requires that statistics be kept regarding the occurrence of bias-related incidents in order to effectively root out and deal with the problem. The federal Hate Crimes Statistics Act of 1990 established a national system for collecting bias crime statistics. The reasoning for this law is to bring greater public attention to the alarming rise in hate crimes, and to more effectively prosecute such crimes.

HATE GROUPS

There are over 300 known "hate groups" in the United States, totalling tens of thousands of members. In addition, many more nonmember citizens follow and support these groups in some way. The most infamous of these hate groups is the "Ku Klux Klan," and the "Aryan" groups, all of which have as their common theme the belief in white supremacy.

The Ku Klux Klan

The Ku Klux Klan is perhaps the most well known of all hate groups. The Ku Klux Klan emerged following the Civil War. The White South attributed the destruction of the southern states' economy to the abolition of slavery. The Ku Klux Klan committed numerous acts of violence, including murder, to create fear in southern Blacks and stop their efforts to exercise any rights.

Out of anger and frustration, many individuals either joined the Ku Klux Klan, or supported the group's activities affirmatively or by non-opposition. Their hatred spread to include other groups, such as Catholics, Jews and immigrants. By 1925, the Ku Klux Klan had a membership exceeding five million Americans.

During the civil rights movement of the 1950's and 1960's, the Ku Klux Klan responded with brutal acts of violence, including murder, bombings and arson. However, because of active criminal and civil prosecution of the Ku Klux Klan, particularly by groups such as the Southern Poverty Law Center as part of their Klan-watch project, membership in the Ku Klux Klan has since dwindled. Nevertheless, there has been no shortage of hate groups ready and willing to take their place and promote bias-related hatred and violence.

Aryan White Supremacist Groups

There are a number of hate groups that surfaced in the late 1980's and early 1990's, many of which use the term "Aryan" in their titles, e.g. "The White Aryan Resistance," "The Aryan Youth Movement," "Aryan Independence," and "Aryan Nations." The Aryans were prehistoric people from Northern Europe who spoke Indo-European. The term "Aryan" as used by these hate groups commonly refers to Caucasian gentiles, and is derived from Nazi ideology that the Aryans are a superior race of people.

These so-called Aryan groups espouse these white supremacy views, and promote violence against non-whites, particularly Jews. They believe that they are the true descendants of Adam and Eve and that all other peoples represent evil. The Aryan groups heed the racist beliefs of mass-murderer Adolf Hitler. They have recruited youths to join in their hate mongering—commonly known as "skinheads"—and have used these youth groups to advance and perpetuate their racist views.

A resource directory for hate crime victims is set forth at Appendix 28.

THE HATE CRIMES PREVENTION ACT OF 1999

The Hate Crimes Prevention Act prohibits anyone from willfully causing bodily injury to any person, or through the use of fire, a firearm, or an explosive device, attempting to cause bodily injury to any person, because of the actual or perceived race, color, religion, or national origin of that person.

Congress determined that the incidence of violence motivated by "hate" directed at the defined groups is divisive, poses a serious national problem, disrupts the tranquility and safety of communities, and negatively impacts interstate commerce in the manner set forth in the Act.

Congress concluded that existing Federal law was inadequate to address the problem and, although state and local jurisdictions will continue to prosecute the vast majority of bias-related crimes, Federal jurisdiction is necessary to supplement state and local jurisdiction and ensure that justice is achieved in each case.

Although the Act, on its face, seeks only to punish the "conduct" of selecting another person for violence because of his or her race, color, national origin, religion, gender, sexual orientation, or disability, there is concern that, in proving the intentional conduct, the prosecution will bring in evidence of the defendant's racial bigotry or association with hate groups.

For example, the prosecutor may introduce racial or other bigoted epithets directed toward the victim by the defendant. Thus, the finder of fact may conclude that the speech-related evidence is a proper basis for proving the intentional selection element of the offense, whether or not it was related to the chain of events leading to the violence. Further, associating the defendant with a particular "hate group" may serve to convict the defendant on a "guilt by association" type theory.

The text of the Hate Crimes Prevention Act of 1999 is set forth at Appendix 29.

CHAPTER 10:
THE EFFECTS OF VICTIMIZATION

IN GENERAL

Studies have concluded that victimization, particularly if the individual is victimized more than once, causes profound effects on the crime victim. Following a traumatic event, many people suffer what is commonly referred to as stress. Of course, being the victim of crime is quite a traumatic event for the victim and his or her family. This is particularly so if the crime was a violent crime.

Stress can be either long-term or short-term. A seriously destructive crime may cause stress in the victim's life for years following the event. Many people who suffer long-term stress are still able to function normally. However, when the stress interferes with one's ability to function, he or she may be suffering from a condition known as post-traumatic stress disorder (PTSD).

Of course, having experienced a traumatic crisis does not necessarily mean the victim will develop post-traumatic stress disorder. Victims who seek crisis intervention—e.g. counseling—early in the healing process have a much better chance of reducing the risk of developing post-traumatic stress disorder.

POST-TRAUMATIC STRESS DISORDER

Post-traumatic stress disorder may affect the actual victim of the crime, as well as the victim's family and close friends, regardless of age or gender. According to the Diagnostic and Statistical Manual of Mental Disorders, post-traumatic stress disorder occurs when a person has been exposed to an extreme traumatic stressor in which both of the following were present:

1. The person:

(a) directly experienced an event or events that involved actual or threatened death or serious injury, or other threat to one's physical integrity; or

(b) witnessed an event or events that involved death, injury, or a threat to the physical integrity of another person; or

(c) learned about unexpected or violent death, serious harm, or threat of death or injury experienced by a family member or other close associate; and

2. The person's response to the event or events involve intense fear, helplessness or horror.

Post-traumatic stress disorder is defined as acute if it lasts for less than three months following the traumatic event. If it persists beyond that period of time, it is perceived to be a chronic condition. There are a number of objective physical symptoms, and psychological symptoms which may indicate that an individual is suffering from post-traumatic stress disorder, as set forth below.

Physical Symptoms

Physical indicators of post-traumatic stress disorder include:

1. Irritability and the inability to control angry outbursts;

2. Inability to fall asleep and frequent awakening during sleep;

3. Inability to concentrate;

4. Easily startled and/or overly cautious.

Psychological Symptoms

Psychological indicators of post-traumatic stress disorder include:

1. Recurrent recollections of the event which cause severe distress, including flashbacks and illusions;

2. Recurrent stressful dreams replaying the traumatic event;

3. Intense psychological or physiological distress when exposed to internal or external stimuli which trigger thoughts or remembrances about the traumatic event, such as the anniversary date of the occurrence;

4. Avoidance of stimuli which are associated with the traumatic event;

5. A general numbness as indicated by attempts to avoid anything associated with the traumatic event, including thoughts, conversations, people, places or things which may trigger a remembrance of the traumatic event;

6. An inability to remember portions of the traumatic event, e.g. mental blocks.

7. Disinterest in activities and/or detachment from persons that formerly held importance in the individual's life;

8. A decrease in the ability to feel emotions experienced prior to the traumatic event;

9. A foreboding feeling about the future, e.g. focus on death or expectation of more traumatic experiences.

The avoidance of stimuli which trigger remembrance of the traumatic event, and the decrease in the ability to feel emotions, are symptoms commonly referred to as psychic numbing. These feelings usually appear soon after the traumatic experience as a defense mechanism in which the victim's mind virtually shuts out any stimuli which would cause the victim further trauma.

Post-traumatic stress disorder may affect all areas of a person's life—social, familial and occupational—and cause the individual an inability to function. The victim often experiences an intense range of emotions, from profound anger and sadness, to general numbness and withdrawal. This in turn could lead to divorce, job loss and other negative consequences stemming from the original traumatic event, as the victim's family, friends and co-workers attempt to cope with the individual's suffering.

Prognosis

The indicators of post-traumatic stress disorder may not manifest themselves until long after the traumatic event. If the symptoms occur six months or longer after the traumatic event, it is known as delayed onset. Sometimes the victim may function normally for a period of time, and then some event, or a certain sound or smell, may trigger stress reactions, and cause the individual to have flashbacks, or relive certain aspects of the traumatic event. This phenomenon can occur from time to time for many years following the traumatic event, and may cause the individual to suffer physical symptoms, such as those associated with intense fear or panic.

Nevertheless, most victims eventually recover from post-traumatic stress disorder, and the severity of the symptoms decrease and disappear over time. Of course, the prognosis of recovery for each individual is dependent on a number of variables—e.g. severity of the crime—and some victims may suffer their entire lifetime. One key factor in whether a victim will recover involves their ability to rebuild their lives and take control. If the trauma is confronted soon after it is experienced, the extent and duration of the psychological and emotional suffering is generally lessened, and the risk of even developing the stress disorder is significantly reduced.

A directory of state psychological associations is set forth at Appendix 30.

Incidence of Post-Traumatic Stress Disorder

In 1977, a study was undertaken by the National Institute of Justice to determine the psychological impact of crime on victims. The individuals who took part in the study had been victims of crime an average of 15 years prior, and had not undergone any type of counseling.

According to the study, 28% of the crime victims subsequently developed crime-related post-traumatic stress disorder and 7.5% were still suffering from the disorder at the time of evaluation.

SECONDARY VICTIMIZATION

A phenomenon known as secondary victimization refers to the aggravation of stress symptoms by those organizations which are in place to assist the victim, such as the criminal justice system, mental health resources, victim compensation programs, and the victim's family and friends etc.

Secondary victimization often occurs when those working in the criminal justice system treat victims in an insensitive manner. The result is a second emotional trauma that can be more harmful than that caused by the original crime, and which serves to prolong the victim's stress disorder.

THE COST OF CRIME TO THE CRIME VICTIM

Based on the National Crime Victimization Survey, in one year, victims of crime suffered $17.6 billion dollars in crime-related costs, including lost wages, medical costs, property damage, and theft of property or money. The crimes involved included robbery, burglary, rape, assault, and stolen vehicles. The average economic loss totalled $524.

Approximately 31% of all crime victims surveyed sustained some type of physical injury. For violent crimes resulting in injury in which medical expenses were known, 65% involved costs of $250 or more, and only 69% of those victims were covered by health insurance or receiving public benefits. Further, the 1.8 million crime victims surveyed lost a total of 6.1 million days from work. Of course, the economic loss to crime victims continues to accrue long after the crime is committed. For example, medical costs, including psychological counseling expenses, are likely to continue for an undetermined period of time.

CHAPTER 11:
VICTIMS' RIGHTS

THE VICTIM

A victim is generally defined as an individual who has suffered some type of loss or injury as a result of a crime. It is a sad reality that the majority of United States citizens have either been victims of crime, or know someone who has been victimized. It is estimated that five out of six people will be the victims of a violent crime at least one time during their life.

REPORT THE CRIME

It is important for the victim of a crime to immediately contact law enforcement authorities. Crimes which are not reported cannot be investigated, and the perpetrators cannot be apprehended. Crimes which are not reported offer little deterrence to criminals who will most likely commit additional crimes until caught. Accurate crime statistics cannot be gathered if crimes go unreported, thus, communities in need of crime prevention resources will not receive adequate protection.

Further, if the crime victim fails to report the crime, they will not be entitled to compensation from the state's compensation fund. Most programs require that the victim report the crime within a certain time period after its occurrence. In addition, if recovery is sought from private insurance, the insurance company will likely require a copy of the police report. Also, it is unlikely that the victim will ever have stolen property returned to them if there is no record made of the theft with law enforcement authorities.

Unfortunately, a substantial number of crimes go unreported. There are a number of reasons why a victim may not report a crime. The most common reasons victims give for non-reporting include (i) fear of reprisal from the criminal; (ii) concern for privacy; (iii) inconvenience;

(iv) relative insignificance of the crime; (v) lack of faith in the system; and (vi) lack of evidence.

THE VICTIMS' RIGHTS MOVEMENT

A victims' rights movement has emerged over the past two decades to champion the rights of crime victims. This movement has been responsible for the passage of important federal, state and local legislation designed to protect the crime victim and his or her family, permit the victim to participate more fully in the criminal proceedings, and provide valuable resources to the victim.

VICTIM ASSISTANCE ORGANIZATIONS

Crime victims often do not know where to turn for help in dealing with the emotional aftermath of the crime. This is particularly so if the crime victim decided, for whatever reason, not to report the crime to law enforcement officials. If the crime is reported, there are generally resources offered through the system. Information is usually provided by the prosecutor's office, the court, or the police department.

Many local communities offer programs to assist the victim, regardless of whether the crime is reported. Such programs are usually listed in the telephone directory under "victim's assistance." Victims of specific crimes may search under their particular category, e.g. "rape crisis lines;" "domestic violence lines," etc.

In addition, assistance may be found by contacting local social services or mental health organizations. Most victims' assistance organizations provide a wide variety of programs, including therapy and counseling; support groups; and practical help and information. For example, assistance may be provided in obtaining compensation from state victim compensation boards, or in completing a victim impact statement.

A resource directory of organizations which assist crime victims is set forth at Appendix 31.

VICTIMS' RIGHTS LEGISLATION

Specific legislation concerning victims' rights is further discussed below. In general, however, laws have been passed in all jurisdictions giving victims certain rights, sometimes referred to as the Victims' Bill of

Rights." Some of the most important provisions of victims' rights legislation include:

1. The right to attend the criminal proceedings, including the trial, the sentencing, and any subsequent parole hearings, and the right to be heard;

2. The right to be notified of each stage of the criminal proceedings so that the victim can participate if he or she wishes to do so;

3. The right to compensation—such as that provided by state victim compensation programs—and restitution by the offender, including the right to recover compensation derived from the criminal's exploitation of the crime;

4. The right to be informed of all available legal remedies, including the right to pursue civil action against the criminal, e.g. to recover punitive damages; and

5. The right to be protected from harassment, including security during the criminal proceedings, and relocation assistance if warranted.

RIGHTS OF THE SURVIVORS OF MURDER VICTIMS

When a family member is murdered, the survivors' only recourse is to the criminal justice system to bring the criminal to justice, and thus provide the family with some closure to the tragedy. Historically, family members were not generally viewed as "victims of the crime," and they had little or no official involvement in the proceedings.

In recent years, this has begun to change, in large part due to the activism of the victims' rights movement. The victims' rights movement has fought to have the family of a homicide victim recognized as victims of the crime who are entitled to actively participate in the criminal proceedings. In fact, many states have enacted laws which consider crime victims to include family members of homicide victims for the purposes of affording them certain rights similar to those afforded the victim.

These rights include the right to notification concerning the criminal proceedings; the right to be protected from harassment; the right to victim compensation and services; and the right to make a victim impact statement.

The Victim Impact Statement

A victim impact statement is a written or oral report which details the manner in which the crime affected the victim and the victim's family. The statement is commonly given at the time of sentencing, and at parole hearings at the time the criminal becomes eligible for parole.

The victim impact statement is usually offered by the victim, or the victim's survivors. In the case of a minor or incompetent victim, the statement may be offered by the parents or legal guardian of the victim. The victim impact statement brings to the court's attention the pain and suffering caused by the crime, which may be expected to endure long after the criminal is sentenced. For example, the statement may describe the physical, mental or financial harm the crime has caused the family.

The victim impact statement also gives the victim and/or the victim's family the chance to participate more fully in the criminal justice process and the quest to bring the criminal to justice. Many states even allow the victim to recommend a sentence or offer comments on the proposed sentence.

Most states have laws which give the victim and/or the victim's family, the right to make a victim impact statement, and require the court or the parole board to consider the statement when rendering a decision. The statement may also be contained in the criminal's presentencing report to the court, and periodically updated and sent to the parole board.

LEGISLATION

Notoriety for Profit—"Son of Sam" Laws

In 1977, New York enacted a statute known as the "Son of Sam" law. "Son of Sam" refers to David Berkowitz—a deranged serial killer who gripped New Yorkers with fear for a period of time during his murderous crime spree. Following his capture and conviction, David Berkowitz was presented with a number of lucrative offers to tell his bizarre story.

In response, New York enacted the "Son of Sam" statute which permits crime victims and their survivors to share in any profits derived from the sale of such a criminal's story. The reasoning for the "Son of Sam" law is to prevent criminals from profiting from their crimes while the victims continue to suffer, and are further subjected to additional exposure as a result of the publicity.

Following in New York's footsteps, the federal government and the majority of states enacted similar statutes. These laws generally provide that when a criminal contracts to receive profits from telling his or her story—e.g. a book or movie deal—the paying party is required to turn over any profits payable to the criminal directly to the state. These funds are then made available to the criminal's victims, and/or placed in the state's victim compensation fund.

Most states require the victim to sue the criminal and obtain a civil judgment for damages as a prerequisite for making a claim under the law. Other states rely on their victim compensation programs to handle the claims. The time limit for suing the criminal and making a claim varies among the jurisdictions. Therefore, the reader is advised to check the law of his or her own jurisdiction in this regard.

Since the enactment of the "Son of Sam" law, there have been constitutional challenges to the law. In 1991, in *Simon & Schuster vs. The New York Crime Victims Board*, The U.S. Supreme Court agreed and found that New York's law is overly broad and violates the constitutional right to free speech under the First Amendment. In response, the New York legislature enacted new legislation. Other states have also amended their "Son of Sam" laws to avoid these laws being struck down as unconstitutional.

Confidentiality Statutes

Legislation exists in most jurisdictions which protects the victim's right to privacy, so as to encourage the reporting of crimes to law enforcement authorities and to protect the victim from secondary victimization by the media.

In particular, due to the nature of the crime, there are specific categories of crime victims entitled to confidentiality, including victims of rape and sexual assault, child victims, and victims of domestic violence. Laws may prohibit the release of the victim's name, address and telephone number, as well as the personal records of the victim, e.g. medical records. Some laws prohibit the media from publishing the victim's likeness or other identifying information, and in some states, those who do so may be liable for damages to the victim.

Title 42 U.S.C. §10606—Rights of Crime Victims

Section (b) of this federal statute affords the crime victim the following rights:

1. The right to be treated with fairness and with respect for the victim's dignity and privacy.

2. The right to be reasonably protected form the accused offender.

3. The right to be notified of court proceedings.

4. The right to be present at all public court proceedings related to the offense, unless the court determines that testimony by the victim would be materially affected if the victim heard other testimony at trial.

5. The right to confer with the attorney for the Government in the case.

6. The right to restitution.

7. The right to information about the conviction, sentencing, imprisonment, and release of the offender.

Further, Section 10606(a) requires that the employees of the Department of Justice and other Federal agencies engaged in the detection, investigation, or prosecution of crime, make their "best efforts" to see that crime victims are accorded the rights described above.

Title 42 U.S.C. §10607—Services to Victims

This federal statute requires that crime victims be informed of their right to receive the following services:

1. Emergency medical and social services;

2. The availability of restitution or other relief to which the victim may be entitled under law, and the manner in which such relief may be obtained;

3. Counseling, treatment and support through available public and private programs;

4. Assistance in contacting the persons who are responsible for providing the above-described services.

Further, the victim is entitled to protection from the suspected offender and any persons acting in concert with the offender. This statute also states that, during the prosecution and trial phase of the proceedings, the crime victim is entitled to certain information, including notice concerning:

1. The status of the investigation of the crime, to the extent it is appropriate to inform the victim and to the extent that it will not interfere with the investigation;

2. The arrest of a suspected offender;

3. The filing of charges against a suspected offender;

4. The scheduling of each court proceeding that the witness is either required to attend or entitled to attend;

5. The release or detention status of an offender or suspected offender;

6. The acceptance of a plea of guilty or nolo contendere or the rendering of a verdict after trial; and

7. The sentence imposed on an offender, including the date on which the offender will be eligible for parole.

Following the trial and conviction of the offender, the victim is entitled to notice of any scheduled parole hearings, and notice of the offender's escape, work release, furlough, any other form of release from custody, or the death of the offender.

THE ROLE OF THE VICTIM

In General

Because the commission of a crime is considered to be an act committed against society, the crime victim is not considered a party to the criminal proceeding. The state basically takes the role as the plaintiff, and the state's attorney prosecutes the case against the criminal—the defendant.

The victim has very little input into the criminal proceeding. He or she cannot force the government to prosecute the criminal if the prosecutor determines that there is not enough evidence. Of course, as further set forth below, the crime victim is entitled to bring a civil action against the criminal to recover damages, and the victim is also entitled under most state laws, to receive compensation from some type of victims' compensation fund.

In the context of the criminal proceeding, the victim's role is basically that of a witness to the crime. The victimization forms the basis for the criminal prosecution of the "social wrong." However, the victim does not have a right to assume any control over the criminal proceedings.

The victim does however have certain basic rights connected with the proceeding, e.g. the right to be present at all stages of the prosecution, and the right to protection from intimidation. In addition, the victim has the right to present a victim impact statement on various occasions—e.g. at sentencing or parole hearings—for the court or parole board to consider when rendering a decision concerning the criminal.

Child Witnesses

The awareness that a child must be treated with sensitivity and care has led to efforts to make a child's participation in the criminal justice system less traumatic. As a result, special rules generally apply when a child is a witness in a criminal case, particularly when there is a potential for emotional trauma. These include:

(i) the use of a child's videotaped witness statements and/or closed circuit testimony rather than live testimony in front of the perpetrator;

(ii) conducting proceedings in a closed courtroom;

(iii) permitting testimony to take place in the judge's chambers; and

(iv) limiting the amount of time a child is required to testify without taking a break.

PURSUING CIVIL REMEDIES

The civil justice system, unlike the criminal justice process, does not rule on the guilt or innocence of the criminal, nor does it subject him or her to criminal penalties, such as incarceration. The goal of the civil justice system is to determine whether the criminal—referred to as the defendant—is civilly liable for the injuries caused by the crime. If the defendant is found to be liable, he or she is generally required to pay monetary damages to the victim or the victim's survivors.

In order to be held liable, the standard of proof is that the defendant be found liable by a preponderance of the evidence. This is a much lower standard than required in a criminal case. Thus, even if the defendant is never prosecuted criminally, or is acquitted in the criminal court, the victim is still permitted to bring a civil action against the defendant.

A crime victim has the right to pursue civil remedies against a criminal for the losses and injuries sustained as a result of the crime committed. Although, as stated above, a criminal conviction is not required in order for a victim to pursue civil remedies, the fact of a conviction in criminal court can be powerful evidence of the criminal's liability in the civil action.

Unfortunately, it is often the case that the criminal is judgment proof, i.e., he or she does not have any financial resources or assets against which a monetary judgment can be enforced. Nevertheless, civil actions have been successfully prosecuted against third parties who may be held jointly responsible for the acts of the criminal, and who do have resources against which a judgment can be satisfied.

For example, if an employer negligently hires an individual who commits a crime during the course of his or her employment, the employer may be held responsible. Another scenario in which a third party could be held responsible occurs if a building owner does not provide adequate security for the tenants. If a crime is committed as a result of the inadequate security, the building owner may be held responsible.

By taking civil action, victims are able to recover monetary damages for such items as pain and suffering, medical expenses, lost wages, and property loss. Nevertheless, winning a monetary judgment does not guarantee payment. Many criminals are judgment proof. The victim is more likely to collect on the judgment from those third parties found responsible through their negligent actions.

VICTIM COMPENSATION

Victim compensation refers to the money paid to a crime victim through state victim assistance programs. Such monies are paid out to try to compensate the crime victim for some of his or her pecuniary losses as a result of the crime.

Although financial relief cannot heal the trauma associated with victimization, it does serve to relieve the victim of further upset associated with monetary pressures, such as loss of income, payment of medical expenses, etc., which can prove devastating.

All of the states and the District of Columbia have established, by statute, some type of victim compensation program. There has not yet been established any similar federal compensation program, although the state programs are often partially federally funded.

A directory of state victim compensation programs is set forth at Appendix 32.

Eligibility

While specific relief may vary, most victim assistance programs are similarly constructed. Of course, the crime victim is the primary recipient of the compensation. This is so whether or not the offender is ever apprehended provided the crime victim follows all of the procedural requirements. In addition, many states also provide compensation to certain family members of homicide victims—known as secondary or derivative victims—as further discussed below.

A table of eligible persons eligible under state victim compensation statutes is set forth at Appendix 33.

Application procedures vary from state to state, but a victim will usually be referred to a victim compensation program by police, prosecutors, or a victim assistance programs. Applications are usually available through law enforcement or victim assistance programs, or by contacting the compensation program directly. The process begins when an application is signed and submitted by the victim or an eligible family member.

The application for compensation must be made within a certain time period following the crime—e.g. two years—in the state where the crime took place. The governing law would also be the state where the crime took place, even if the victim's home state would provide greater compensation. The types of crimes which are compensable vary among the states. Serious offenses, such as felonies, are usually covered by the statutes.

A table of compensable crimes under state victim compensation statutes is set forth at Appendix 34.

Limitations on Eligibility

Depending on the specific circumstances surrounding the crime, most states have placed limitations on eligibility. Although state statutes may vary, the most common situations in which a primary or secondary victim would be denied compensation benefits are set forth below.

1. A victim who was involved in the commission of a crime at the time he or she was victimized is not eligible for compensation.

2. Victims who do not cooperate with law enforcement officials in the criminal proceedings are not entitled to compensation.

3. Victims who do not meet a state-mandated financial needs test are not entitled to compensation.

4. Victims who have had their expenses covered by other sources, such as insurance coverage, are not entitled to duplicate compensation.

Necessity of Proof

Most victim compensation statutes require the victims to provide proof of their losses, such as medical bills, funeral bills, and proof of lost income, before they will compensate the victim. In addition, the victim must have reported the crime to law enforcement authorities, usually within 24 to 48 hours of its occurrence. Nevertheless, there is no requirement that the criminal be convicted, or that he or she is ever arrested for the crime.

Covered Expenses

Most victim compensation statutes provide compensation to the victim for the items listed below, up to a statutory maximum amount:

1. Medical expenses, which comprises over fifty percent of all claims;

2. Lost wages, which is the second largest category of payments made;

3. Financial support for dependent family members of a homicide victim;

4. Funeral expenses; and

5. Necessary psychological treatment and counseling.

Some victim compensation programs also cover the following costs:

1. Moving or relocation expenses where the victim is in imminent physical danger, or if the move is medically necessary due to the injuries sustained;

2. Transportation to medical providers when the provider is located in a place distant from the victim's residence, or when there exist other special circumstances;

3. Replacement services for work the victim is unable to perform because of crime-related injury, such as child care and housekeeping, generally limited to payments to non-family members;

4. Crime-scene cleanup, or the cost of securing a home or restoring it to its pre-crime condition;

5. Rehabilitation, which may include physical therapy and/or job therapy;

6. Modifications to homes or vehicles for paralyzed victims; and

7. Fees for attorneys who are hired to help the victim with the application process, generally in limited amounts.

A small minority of states will compensate victims for their "pain and suffering." However, most victims are advised to file a civil lawsuit against the offender or any negligent third parties to recover monetary damages for pain and suffering.

Maximum benefits available to victims from the state victim compensation programs generally range between $10,000 and $25,000, though a few states have higher maximums. Many states are seeking to raise benefit levels through legislative change.

A table setting forth the maximum compensation available under state victim compensation statutes is set forth at Appendix 35.

Surviving Family Members

Many state victim compensation programs provide financial assistance to the family members of homicide victims. Depending on the state, such compensation may include financial losses or expenses which resulted from the death of the victim, including:

1. Medical expenses and burial costs of the victim;

2. Financial support of the crime victim's surviving financially dependent family members;

3. Mental health resources including the cost of psychological counseling related to the trauma of the loss;

In addition, the court may order the offender to provide restitution to the surviving family members for any financial losses they suffered as a result of the loss of their loved one. However, these statutes do not generally provide the right to punitive damages. Thus, the family members must pursue a civil action for wrongful death to recover such damages, as further discussed above.

Collateral Source Payments

Collateral source payments refer to benefits available to a victim through sources such as medical insurance, automobile insurance, Medicaid, Medicare, Social Security, employee benefit plans, etc. All state victim compensation programs require the victim to seek payments from any such available source before it will consider making any payments through the compensation program.

If the victim receives any payment through the compensation program, and subsequently recovers any money from any other source, including the offender, the compensation program must be paid back for whatever portion of the expenses the program covered. An exception exists if the victim's total losses exceed the amount paid by the compensation program plus money received from any other sources.

VICTIM RESTITUTION

Restitution refers to the requirement that the individual who caused harm to the victim must repay the victim. Restitution differs from compensation in several respects. First, the offender must be convicted of the crime for the court to take any type of punitive measures. Restitution must be made by the criminal, who more than likely does not have the resources to pay the victim.

In the past, restitution has largely been ignored as an appropriate remedy, in favor of focusing on punishing the criminal. In large part due to the emergence of the victims' rights movement, restitution has once again been recognized as an invaluable method to hold the offender accountable for his or her crime.

Statutorily-Prescribed Restitution

There has always existed a common law right to require restitution from the one who has caused harm as a result of a crime. Most states have also enacted legislation which allows for restitution, and many courts now use restitution as a condition of probation. Failure of the criminal to make restitution can result in the revocation of his or her probation. Many states also require restitution and, in cases where restitution is not ordered, those states require the court to state its reasons for not doing so.

Eligibility

Of course, restitution can only be ordered if the offender is apprehended and convicted, unlike victim compensation which can be applied for whether or not the criminal is ever caught. All primary victims of a crime are eligible for restitution. Many states also permit the surviving family members of a homicide victim to recover for the cost associated with the victim's loss, such as medical expenses and funeral costs.

Covered Expenses

Most statutes provide restitution to the victim for the items listed below, which may include:

1. Out-of-pocket costs such as medical expenses and the cost of psychological counseling;

2. The cost of property damage; and

3. Lost wages.

The Court generally specifies the amount of the restitution to be paid, and the manner of payment. However, if the defendant is not able to pay, the court may not be permitted to order more than what would be reasonable considering the offender's financial resources. If the offender does not comply with the restitution order, he or she may be subject to incarceration, and if the offender is on probation, his or her probation may be revoked.

This chapter sets forth an overview of the rights afforded victims of crime and violence. A more detailed discussion of this topic may be found in this author's legal almanac entitled *Victim's Rights Law* also published by Oceana Publishing Company.

APPENDIX 1:
TYPE OF WEAPON USED, BY AGE OF VICTIMS (1993 - 2001)

AGE OF VICTIM	NO WEAPON	ANY WEAPON	FIREARM	SHARP OBJECT	BLUNT OBJECT/OTHER	WEAPON TYPE UNKNOWN
12-14	77.2%	17.9%	2.6%	6.3%	9.0%	4.9%
15-17	67.3%	25.1%	8.9%	6.5%	9.7%	7.6%
18-20	62.6%	30.1%	12.6%	7.1%	10.5%	7.3%
21-24	63.7%	28.8%	11.9%	7.6%	9.3%	7.5%
25-34	64.5%	27.4%	10.3%	6.4%	10.7%	8.1%
35-49	64.9%	25.5%	9.8%	5.7%	9.9%	9.6%
50-64	63.4%	24.9%	9.1%	5.5%	10.2%	11.7%
65 or Older	54.4%	30.4%	13.1%	6.1%	11.2%	15.2%

Source: U.S. Department of Justice, Bureau of Justice Statistics.

APPENDIX 2:
MURDER RATE OF CHILDREN UNDER AGE 12, BY WEAPON USED (1993 - 2001)

TYPE OF WEAPON	AVERAGE ANNUAL NUMBER	PERCENTAGE (%)	RATE PER 100,000 CHILDREN
No Weapon	399	45.3%	0.9
Any Weapon	356	40.5%	0.8
Firearm	141	16%	0.3
Knife/Sharp Object	40	4.6%	0.1
Blunt Object	56	6.3%	0.1
Other Weapon	120	13.6%	0.3

Source: U.S. Department of Justice, Bureau of Justice Statistics.

APPENDIX 3:
TYPE OF WEAPON USED,
VICTIM/OFFENDER RELATIONSHIP TYPE
(1993 - 2001)

TYPE OF WEAPON	INTIMATES	KNOWN NON-INTIMATE	STRANGERS
No Weapon	80%	75%	56%
Any Weapon	16%	20%	33%
Firearm	5%	5%	14%
Sharp Object	4%	6%	7%
Blunt Object/Other	7%	9%	11%
Weapon Type Unknown	4%	5%	11%

Source: U.S. Department of Justice, Bureau of Justice Statistics.

APPENDIX 4:
INJURIES SUFFERED FROM VIOLENT VICTIMIZATIONS, BY TYPE OF WEAPON USED (1993 - 2001)

TYPE OF CRIME	TYPE OF WEAPON	NO INJURY	SERIOUS INJURY	MILD INJURY
RAPE/SEXUAL ASSAULT	No Weapon	48.4%	1.7%	19.9%
	Any weapon	24.8%	10.1%	35%
ROBBERY	No Weapon	64.3%	3.1%	32.6%
	Any Weapon	72.8%	8.5%	18.7%
	Firearm	83.6%	4.2%	12.2%
	Knife/Sharp Object	69.1%	13.5%	17.4%
	Blunt Object/Other	48.9%	13.8%	37.3%
ASSAULT	No Weapon	76%	1.8%	22.3%
	Any Weapon	74.9%	7.0%	18.2%
	Firearm	87%	4.8%	8.1%
	Knife/Sharp Object	74.5%	12.3%	13.2%
	Blunt Object/Other	66.2%	5.6%	28.2%

Source: U.S. Department of Justice Bureau of Justice Statistics.

APPENDIX 5:
VICTIMS' METHODS OF SELF-DEFENSE TO VIOLENT CRIME (1993 - 2001)

VICTIM RESPONSE	PERCENTAGE OF TIME (%)
Offered no resistance	39.3%
Used physical force toward offender	13%
Attacked/threatened offender without a weapon	10.8%
Attacked/threatened offender with a gun	0.7%
Attacked/threatened offender with other weapon	1.4%
Resisted or captured offender	15%
Scared or warned off offender	4.2%
Persuaded or appeased offender	5.5%
Escaped/hid/got away	9.8%
Got help or gave alarm	3.9%
Reacted to pain or emotion	0.3%
Other	8.9%
Method of resistance unknown	0.2%

Source: U.S. Department of Justice& Bureau of Justice Statistics.

APPENDIX 6:
TYPE OF WEAPON USED, BY VICTIM'S ACTIVITY AT TIME OF INCIDENT
(1993 - 2001)

ACTIVITY	NO WEAPON	ANY WEAPON	FIREARM	SHARP OBJECT	BLUNT OBJECT/OTHER	WEAPON TYPE UNKNOWN
Work	19.8%	14.5%	15%	16%	13%	14.5%
School	11.3%	2.8%	1.1%	4.6%	3.3%	4.6%
Home	23.8%	20.5%	18.4%	23.2%	20.7%	17.9%
Shopping	3.1%	4.7%	5.6%	4.8%	3.8%	6.3%
Leisure away from home	21%	26.9%	26.6%	25.1%	28.4%	24.5%
Traveling to or from work	13.6%	22.9%	25.4%	18.6%	23.2%	25%
Other	7.4%	7.8%	7.9%	7.7%	7.7%	7.2%

Source: U.S. Department of Justice, Bureau of Justice Statistics.

APPENDIX 7:
TYPE OF WEAPON USED, BY TIME OF DAY
(1993 - 2001)

TYPE OF WEAPON	DAY	NIGHT
No weapon	71%	62%
Any weapon	21%	30%
Firearm	6%	12%
Sharp Object	6%	7%
Blunt Object/Other	9%	11%
Weapon Type Unknown	8%	8%

Source: U.S. Department of Justice, Bureau of Justice Statistics.

APPENDIX 8:
PERCENTAGE OF WEAPON USE REPORTED, BY TYPE
OF VIOLENT CRIME
(1993 – 2001)

TYPE OF WEAPON	HOMICIDE	RAPE/SEXUAL ASSAULT	ROBBERY	ALL ASSAULTS
Firearm	70%	3%	27%	8%
Knife/Sharp Object	13%	3%	13%	6%
Blunt Object	5%	1%	5%	4%
Other	3%	1%	5%	6%
Weapon Type Unknown	4%	7%	11%	8%
No Weapon	4%	85%	39%	69%

Source: U.S. Department of Justice, Bureau of Justice Statistics.

APPENDIX 9:
RESOURCE DIRECTORY FOR CHILD
VICTIMS OF VIOLENCE

NAME	ADDRESS	TELEPHONE NUMBER
American Association for Protecting Children	P.O. Box 1266, Denver, CO 80231	800-227-5242
American Bar Association Center on Children and the Law	1800 M Street N.W., Suite 200-S, Washington, DC 20036	202-331-2250
American Professional Society on the Abuse of Children	969 East 60th Street, Chicago, IL 60637	312-702-9419
Children of Murdered Parents	P.O. Box 9317, Whittier, CA 90608	310-699-8427
Council for the Prevention of Child Abuse and Neglect	1305 Fourth Avenue, Room 202, Seattle, WA 98101	206-343-2590
Mothers Against Drunk Driving	511 East John Carpenter Freeway, Suite 700, Irving, TX 75062	800-438-MADD
National Adolescent Sexual Abuse Prevention Project	124D Senatorial Drive, Wilmington, DE 19807	302-654-1102
National Center on Child Abuse and Neglect, U.S. Department of Health and Human Services	P.O. Box 1182, Washington, DC 20013	202-619-0257
Juvenile Justice Clearinghouse	1600 Research Boulevard, Rockville, MD 20850	800-638-8736
National Center for the Prosecution of Child Abuse	1033 North Fairfax Street, Suite 200, Alexandria, VA 22314	703-739-0321

NAME	ADDRESS	TELEPHONE NUMBER
National Child Abuse Coalition	733 Fifteenth Street N.W., Suite 938, Washington, DC 20005	202-247-3666
National Child Abuse Hotline	P.O. Box 630, Hollywood, CA 90028	800-4A-CHILD
National Council on Child Abuse and Family Violence	1155 Connecticut Avenue N.W., Suite 300, Washington, DC 20036	202-429-6695
National Council of Juvenile and Family Court Judges	P.O. Box 8970, Reno, NV 89507	702-784-6012
National Organization of Parents of Murdered Children	100 East Eighth Street, Suite B-41, Cincinnati, OH 45202	513-721-5683
Students Against Driving Drunk	P.O. Box 800, Marlboro, MA 01752	508-481-3568

APPENDIX 10:
THE CHILD PORNOGRAPHY PROTECTION ACT OF 1996

PUBLIC LAW 104-208 (SEPTEMBER 30, 1996)

SECTION 2252A. CERTAIN ACTIVITIES RELATING TO MATERIAL CONSTITUTING OR CONTAINING CHILD PORNOGRAPHY

(a) Any person who—

(1) knowingly mails, or transports or ships in interstate or foreign commerce by any means, including by computer, any child pornography;

(2) knowingly receives or distributes—

(A) any child pornography that has been mailed, or shipped or transported in interstate or foreign commerce by any means, including by computer; or

(B) any material that contains child pornography that has been mailed, or shipped or transported in interstate or foreign commerce by any means, including by computer;

(3) knowingly reproduces any child pornography for distribution through the mails, or in interstate or foreign commerce by any means, including by computer;

(4) either—

(A) in the special maritime and territorial jurisdiction of the United States, or on any land or building owned by, leased to, or otherwise used by or under the control of the United States Government, or in the Indian country (as defined in section 1151), knowingly sells or possesses with the intent to sell any child pornography; or

(B) knowingly sells or possesses with the intent to sell any child pornography that has been mailed, or shipped or transported in interstate or foreign commerce by any means, including by computer, or that was produced using materials that have been mailed, or shipped or transported in interstate or foreign commerce by any means, including by computer; or

(5) either—

(A) in the special maritime and territorial jurisdiction of the United States, or on any land or building owned by, leased to, or otherwise used by or under the control of the United States Government, or in the Indian country (as defined in section 1151), knowingly possesses any book, magazine, periodical, film, videotape, computer disk, or any other material that contains 3 or more images of child pornography; or

(B) knowingly possesses any book, magazine, periodical, film, videotape, computer disk, or any other material that contains 3 or more images of child pornography that has been mailed, or shipped or transported in interstate or foreign commerce by any means, including by computer, or that was produced using materials that have been mailed, or shipped or transported in interstate or foreign commerce by any means, including by computer, shall be punished as provided in subsection (b).

(b)(1) Whoever violates, or attempts or conspires to violate, paragraphs (1), (2), (3), or (4) of subsection (a) shall be fined under this title or imprisoned not more than 15 years, or both, but, if such person has a prior conviction under this chapter or chapter 109A, or under the laws of any State relating to aggravated sexual abuse, sexual abuse, or abusive sexual conduct involving a minor or ward, or the production, possession, receipt, mailing, sale, distribution, shipment, or transportation of child pornography, such person shall be fined under this title and imprisoned for not less than 5 years nor more than 30 years.

(b)(2) Whoever violates, or attempts or conspires to violate, subsection (a)(5) shall be fined under this title or imprisoned not more than 5 years, or both, but, if such person has a prior conviction under this chapter or chapter 109A, or under the laws of any State relating to the possession of child pornography, such person shall be fined under this title and imprisoned for not less than 2 years nor more than 10 years.

(c) It shall be an affirmative defense to a charge of violating paragraphs (1), (2), (3), or (4) of subsection (a) that—

(1) the alleged child pornography was produced using an actual person or persons engaging in sexually explicit conduct;

(2) each such person was an adult at the time the material was produced; and

(3) the defendant did not advertise, promote, present, describe, or distribute the material in such a manner as to convey the impression that it is or contains a visual depiction of a minor engaging in sexually explicit conduct.

(b) TECHNICAL AMENDMENT—The table of sections for chapter 110 of title 18, United States Code, is amended by adding after the item relating to section 2252 the following:

'2252A. Certain activities relating to material constituting or containing child pornography.'

APPENDIX 11:
JACOB WETTERLING CRIMES AGAINST CHILDREN AND SEXUALLY VIOLENT OFFENDER REGISTRATION ACT

TITLE XVII-CRIMES AGAINST CHILDREN

Subtitle A—Jacob Wetterling Crimes Against Children and Sexually Violent Offender Registration Act

SEC. 170101. ESTABLISHMENT OF PROGRAM.

(a) In General.—

(1) State guidelines.—The Attorney General shall establish guidelines for State programs that require—

(A) a person who is convicted of a criminal offense against a victim who is a minor or who is convicted of a sexually violent offense to register a current address with a designated State law enforcement agency for the time period specified in subparagraph (A) of subsection (b)(6); and

(B) a person who is a sexually violent predator to register a current address with a designated State law enforcement agency unless such requirement is terminated under subparagraph (B) of subsection (b)(6).

(2) Court determination.—A determination that a person is a sexually violent predator and a determination that a person is no longer a sexually violent predator shall be made by the sentencing court after receiving a report by a State board composed of experts in the field of the behavior and treatment of sexual offenders.

(3) Definitions.—For purposes of this section:

(A) The term "criminal offense against a victim who is a minor" means any criminal offense that consists of—

(i) kidnapping of a minor, except by a parent;

(ii) false imprisonment of a minor, except by a parent;

(iii) criminal sexual conduct toward a minor;

(iv) solicitation of a minor to engage in sexual conduct;

(v) use of a minor in a sexual performance;

(vi) solicitation of a minor to practice prostitution;

(vii) any conduct that by its nature is a sexual offense against a minor; or

(viii) an attempt to commit an offense described in any of clauses (i) through (vii), if the State—

(I) makes such an attempt a criminal offense; and

(II) chooses to include such an offense in those which are criminal offenses against a victim who is a minor for the purposes of this section. For purposes of this subparagraph conduct which is criminal only because of the age of the victim shall not be considered a criminal offense if the perpetrator is 18 years of age or younger.

(B) The term "sexually violent offense" means any criminal offense that consists of aggravated sexual abuse or sexual abuse (as described in sections 2241 and 2242 of title 18, United States Code, or as described in the State criminal code) or an offense that has as its elements engaging in physical contact with another person with intent to commit aggravated sexual abuse or sexual abuse (as described in such sections of title 18, United States Code, or as described in the State criminal code).

(C) The term "sexually violent predator" means a person who has been convicted of a sexually violent offense and who suffers from a mental abnormality or personality disorder that makes the person likely to engage in predatory sexually violent offenses.

(D) The term "mental abnormality" means a congenital or acquired condition of a person that affects the emotional or volitional capacity of the person in a manner that predisposes that person to the commission of criminal sexual acts to a degree that makes the person a menace to the health and safety of other persons.

(E) The term "predatory" means an act directed at a stranger, or a person with whom a relationship has been established or promoted for the primary purpose of victimization.

(b) Registration Requirement Upon Release, Parole, Supervised Release, or Probation.—

An approved State registration program established under this section shall contain the following elements:

(1) Duty of state prison official or court.—

(A) If a person who is required to register under this section is released from prison, or placed on parole, supervised release, or probation, a State prison officer, or in the case of probation, the court, shall—

(i) inform the person of the duty to register and obtain the information required for such registration;

(ii) inform the person that if the person changes residence address, the person shall give the new address to a designated State law enforcement agency in writing within 10 days;

(iii) inform the person that if the person changes residence to another State, the person shall register the new address with the law enforcement agency with whom the person last registered, and the person is also required to register with a designated law enforcement agency in the new State not later than 10 days after establishing residence in the new State, if the new State has a registration requirement;

(iv) obtain fingerprints and a photograph of the person if these have not already been obtained in connection with the offense that triggers registration; and

(v) require the person to read and sign a form stating that the duty of the person to register under this section has been explained.

(B) In addition to the requirements of subparagraph (A), for a person required to register under subparagraph (B) of subsection (a)(1), the State prison officer or the court, as the case may be, shall obtain the name of the person, identifying factors, anticipated future residence, offense history, and documentation of any treatment received for the mental abnormality or personality disorder of the person.

(2) Transfer of information to state and the FBI.—

The officer, or in the case of a person placed on probation, the court, shall, within 3 days after receipt of information described in paragraph (1), forward it to a designated State law enforcement agency. The State law enforcement agency shall immediately enter the information into the appropriate State law enforcement record system and notify the appropriate law enforcement agency having jurisdiction where the person expects to reside. The State law enforcement agency shall also immediately transmit the conviction data and fingerprints to the Federal Bureau of Investigation.

(3) Verification.—

(A) For a person required to register under subparagraph (A) of subsection (a)(1), on each anniversary of the person's initial registration date during the period in which the person is required to register under this section the following applies:

(i) The designated State law enforcement agency shall mail a nonforwardable verification form to the last reported address of the person.

(ii) The person shall mail the verification form to the designated State law enforcement agency within 10 days after receipt of the form.

(iii) The verification form shall be signed by the person, and state that the person still resides at the address last reported to the designated State law enforcement agency.

(iv) If the person fails to mail the verification form to the designated State law enforcement agency within 10 days after receipt of the form, the person shall be in violation of this section unless the person proves that the person has not changed the residence address.

(B) The provisions of subparagraph (A) shall be applied to a person required to register under subparagraph (B) of subsection (a)(1), except that such person must verify the registration every 90 days after the date of the initial release or commencement of parole.

(4) Notification of local law enforcement agencies of changes in address.—

A change of address by a person required to register under this section reported to the designated State law enforcement agency shall be immediately reported to the appropriate law enforcement agency having jurisdiction where the person is residing. The designated law enforcement agency shall, if the person changes residence to another State, notify the law enforcement agency with which the person must register in the new State, if the new State has a registration requirement.

(5) Registration for change of address to another state.—

A person who has been convicted of an offense which requires registration under this section shall register the new address with a designated law enforcement agency in another State to which the person moves not later than 10 days after such person establishes residence in the new State, if the new State has a registration requirement.

(6) Length of registration.—

(A) A person required to register under subparagraph (A) of subsection (a)(1) shall continue to comply with this section until 10 years have elapsed since the person was released from prison, placed on parole, supervised release, or probation.

(B) The requirement of a person to register under subparagraph (B) of subsection (a)(1) shall terminate upon a determination, made in accordance with paragraph (2) of subsection (a), that the person no longer suffers from a mental abnormality or personality disorder that would make the person likely to engage in a predatory sexually violent offense.

(c) Penalty.—

A person required to register under a State program established pursuant to this section who knowingly fails to so register and keep such registration current shall be subject to criminal penalties in any State in which the person has so failed.

(d) Release of Information.—

The information collected under a State registration program shall be treated as private data except that—

(1) such information may be disclosed to law enforcement agencies for law enforcement purposes;

(2) such information may be disclosed to government agencies conducting confidential background checks; and

(3) the designated State law enforcement agency and any local law enforcement agency authorized by the State agency may release relevant information that is necessary to protect the public concerning a specific person required to register under this section, except that the identity of a victim of an offense that requires registration under this section shall not be released.

(e) Immunity for Good Faith Conduct.—

Law enforcement agencies, employees of law enforcement agencies, and State officials shall be immune from liability for good faith conduct under this section.

(f) Compliance.—

(1) Compliance date.—

Subject to paragraph (2), each State shall have not more than 3 years from the date of enactment of this Act in which to implement this section, except that the Attorney General may grant an additional 2 years to a State that is making good faith efforts to implement this section.

(2) Ineligibility for funds.—

(A) A State that fails to implement the program as described in this section shall not receive 10 percent of the funds that would otherwise be allocated to the State under section 506 of the Omnibus Crime Control and Safe Streets Act of 1968 (42 U.S.C. 3765).

(B) Reallocation of funds.—

Any funds that are not allocated for failure to comply with this section shall be reallocated to States that comply with this section.

APPENDIX 12:
MEGAN'S LAW

SECTION 1. SHORT TITLE.

This Act may be cited as "Megan's Law".

SECTION 2. RELEASE OF INFORMATION AND CLARIFICATION OF PUBLIC NATURE OF INFORMATION.

Section 170101(d) of the Violent Crime Control and Law Enforcement Act of 1994 (42 U.S.C. 14071(d)) is amended to read as follows:

"(d) Release of Information.—

"(1) The information collected under a State registration program may be disclosed for any purpose permitted under the laws of the State.

"(2) The designated State law enforcement agency and any local law enforcement agency authorized by the State agency shall release relevant information that is necessary to protect the public concerning a specific person required to register under this section, except that the identity of a victim of an offense that requires registration under this section shall not be released."

APPENDIX 13:
RESOURCE DIRECTORY FOR ELDERLY VICTIMS OF VIOLENCE

NAME	ADDRESS	TELEPHONE NUMBER
American Association of Retired Persons, Division of Criminal Justice	1909 K Street N.W., Washington, DC 20049	202-728-4363
American Bar Association Commission on Legal Problems of the Elderly	1800 M Street N.W., Suite 200, Washington, DC 20036	202-331-2297
Center for Social Gerontology	117 North First Street, Suite 204, Ann Arbor, MI 48104	313-665-1126
Clearinghouse on Abuse and Neglect of the Elderly	University of Delaware, Newark, DE 19716	302-451-2940
The Gerontological Society	1411 K Street N.W., Suite 300, Washington, DC 20005	202-393-1411
Gray Panthers	311 S. Juniper Street, Suite 601, Philadelphia, PA 19107	215-545-6555
Legal Services for the Elderly	132 W. 43rd Street, 3rd Floor, New York, NY 10036	212-595-1340
National Aging Resource Center on Elder Abuse	810 First Street N.E., Suite 500, Washington, DC 20002	202-682-2470
National Association of Area Agencies on Aging	600 Maryland Avenue S.W., Suite 208, Washington, DC 20024	202-484-7520

NAME	ADDRESS	TELEPHONE NUMBER
National Association of State Units on Aging	600 Maryland Avenue S.W., Suite 208, Washington, DC 20024	202-484-7182
National Council of Senior Citizens	925 15th Street, N.W., Washington, DC 20005	203-347-8800
National Council on the Aging	600 Maryland Avenue S.W., West Wing, Suite 100, Washington, DC 20024	202-479-1200
National Indian Council on Aging	P.O. Box 2088, Albuquerque, NM 87103	505-242-9505
National Pacific/Asian Resource Center on Aging	2033 6th Avenue, Suite 410, Seattle, WA 98121	206-448-0313
National Senior Citizens Law Center	1052 W. 6th Street, 7th Floor, Los Angeles, CA 90017	213-482-3550
National Senior Citizens Law Center	2025 M Street N.W., Suite 400, Washington, DC 20036	202-887-5280

APPENDIX 14:
DIRECTORY OF STATE OFFICES OF THE AGING

STATE	ADDRESS	TELEPHONE NUMBER
Alabama	Commission on Aging, 770 Washington Avenue, Suite 470, Montgomery, AL 36130	205-242-5743
Alaska	Older Alaskans Commission, Pouch C, Mail Stop 0209, Juneau, AK 99811	907-465-3250
Arizona	Aging and Adult Administration, 1400 West Washington Street, Phoenix, AZ 85005	602-542-4446
Arkansas	Arkansas State Office on Aging, Donaghey Building, 7th and Main Streets Little Rock, AR 72201	501-682-2441
California	Department of Aging, 1600 K Street, Sacramento, CA 95814	916-322-5290
Colorado	Aging and Adult Services Division, 1575 Sherman Street, Denver, CO 80220	303-866-3851
Connecticut	Department on Aging, 175 Main Street, Hartford, CT 06106	203-566-3238
Delaware	Division of Aging, 1901 North Dupont Highway, New Castle, DE 19720	302-421-6791
District of Columbia	Office on Aging, 1424 K Street N.W., Washington, DC 20005	202-724-5626

STATE	ADDRESS	TELEPHONE NUMBER
Florida	Program Office of Aging and Adult Services, 1317 Winewood Boulevard, Tallahassee, FL 32301	904-488-8922
Georgia	Office of Aging, 878 Peachtree Street N.E., Room 632 Atlanta, GA 30309	404-894-5333
Hawaii	Executive Office on Aging, 1149 Bethel Street, Room 307 Honolulu, HI 96813	808-548-2593
Idaho	Office on Aging, State House, Room 108, Boise, ID 83720	208-334-3833
Illinois	Department on Aging, 421 East Capitol Avenue, Springfield, IL 62706	217-785-2870
Indiana	Department on Aging & Community Services, 251 N. Illinois Street, Indianapolis, IN 46204	317-232-7020
Iowa	Commission on Aging, 914 Grand Avenue, Suite 236 Jewett Building, Des Moines, IA 50319	515-281-5187
Kansas	Department of Aging, 915 Southwest Harrison, Topeka, KS 66612	913-296-4986
Kentucky	Division for Aging Services, 275 East Main Street, 6th Floor Frankfort, KY 40601	502-564-6930
Louisiana	Office of Elderly Affairs, 4550 North Boulevard, Baton Rouge, LA 70898	504-925-1700
Maine	Bureau of Maine's Elderly, State House, Station No. 11, Augusta, ME 04333	207-626-5335
Maryland	Office on Aging, 301 West Preston Street, Baltimore, MD 21201	301-225-1100
Massachusetts	Department of Elder Affairs, 38 Chauncy Street, Boston, MA 02111	617-727-7750
Michigan	Office of Services to the Aging, P.O. Box 30026, Lansing, MI 48909	517-373-8230

STATE	ADDRESS	TELEPHONE NUMBER
Minnesota	Minnesota Board on Aging, 444 Lafayette Road, St. Paul, MN 55155	612-296-2770
Mississippi	Mississippi Council on Aging, 421 West Pascagoula Street, Jackson, MS 39203	601-354-6590
Missouri	Division on Aging, 615 Howerton Court, Jefferson City, MO 65102	314-751-3082
Montana	The Governor's Office on Aging, State Capitol Building, Capitol Station, Room 219, Helena, MT 59620	406-444-3111
Nebraska	Department on Aging, 301 Centennial Mall South, Lincoln, NE 68509	402-471-2306
Nevada	Division of Aging Services, 340 North 11th Street, Suite 114, Las Vegas, NV 89101	702-486-3545
New Hampshire	Division of Elderly and Adult Services, 6 Hazen Drive, Concord, NH 03301	603-271-4680
New Jersey	Division on Aging, South Broad and Front Streets, Trenton, NJ 08625	609-292-4833
New Mexico	State Agency on Aging, 224 East Palace Avenue, 4th Floor Santa Fe, NM 87501	505-827-7640
New York	Office for the Aging, Empire State Plaza, Agency Building No. 2, Albany, NY 12223,	518-474-4425
North Carolina	Division of Aging, 693 Palmer Drive, Suite 200 Raleigh, NC 27603	919-733-3983
North Dakota	Aging Services, State Capitol Building, Bismarck, ND 58505	701-224-2577
Ohio	Department of Aging, 50 West Broad Street, 9th Floor, Columbus, OH 43215	614-466-5500
Oklahoma	Special Unit on Aging, P.O. Box 25352, Oklahoma City, OK 73125	405-521-2327
Oregon	Oregon Senior Services Division, 313 Public Service Building, Salem, OR 97310	503-378-4728

STATE	ADDRESS	TELEPHONE NUMBER
Pennsylvania	Department of Aging, 231 State Street, Room 307, Harrisburg, PA 17120	717-783-1550
Rhode Island	Department of Elderly Affairs, 160 Pine Street, Providence, RI 02903	401-277-2858
South Carolina	Commission on Aging, 400 Arbor Lake Drive, Suite B-500 Columbia, SC 29223	803-735-0210
South Dakota	Office of Adult Services and Aging, 700 North Illinois Street, Pierre, SD 57501	605-773-3656
Tennessee	Commission on Aging, 706 Church Street, Suite 201, Nashville, TN 37243	615-741-2056
Texas	Department on Aging, P.O. Box 12786, Capitol Station Austin, TX 78741	512-444-2727
Utah	Division of Aging and Adult Services, 120 North - 200 West, Box 45500 Salt Lake City, UT 84145	801-538-3910
Vermont	Office on Aging, 103 South Main Street, Waterbury, VT 05676	802-241-2400
Virginia	Office on Aging, 700 East Franklin Street, Richmond, VA 23219	804-225-2271
Washington	Bureau of Aging and Adult Services, Department of Social and, Health Services, OB-44A, Olympia, WA 98504	206-586-3768
West Virginia	Commission on Aging, State Capitol, Charleston, WV 25305	304-348-3317
Wisconsin	Bureau on Aging, 217 South Hamilton Street, Suite 300 Madison, WI 53707	608-266-2536
Wyoming	Commission on Aging, Hathaway Building, Room 139 Cheyenne, WY 82002	307-777-7986

APPENDIX 15:
DIRECTORY OF NATIONAL
ORGANIZATIONS FOR THE ELDERLY

NAME	ADDRESS	TELEPHONE NUMBER
American Association of Retired Persons	1909 K Street NW, Washington, DC, 20049	202-872-4700
American Society of Aging	833 Market Street, Suite 516, San Francisco, CA 94103	415-543-2617
Choice in Dying	200 Varick Street, New York, NY 10014	212-366-5540
The Gerontological Society of America	1411 K Street NW, Suite 300, Washington, DC 20005	202-393-1411
Gray Panthers	311 S. Juniper Street, Suite 601, Philadelphia, PA 19107	215-545-6555
National Association of Area Agencies on Aging	600 Maryland Avenue SW, West Wing, Suite 208, Washington, DC 20024	202-484-7520
National Association of Retired Federal Employees	1533 New Hampshire Avenue, NW Washington, DC 20036	202-234-0832
National Association of State Units on Aging	600 Maryland Avenue SW, Suite 208, Washington, DC 20024	202-484-7182
National Caucus and Center on Black Aged	1424 K Street, NW, Suite 500, Washington, DC 20005	202-637-8400
National Center on Rural Aging	600 Maryland Avenue SW, West Wing, Suite 100, Washington, DC 20024	202-479-1200

NAME	ADDRESS	TELEPHONE NUMBER
National Citizens Coalition on Nursing Home Reform	1424 16th Street NW, Suite L2, Washington, DC 20036	202-797-0657
National Council of Senior Citizens	925 15th Street, NW, Washington, DC 20005	203-347-8800
National Council on the Aging	600 Maryland Avenue SW, West Wing, Suite 100, Washington, DC 20024	202-479-1200
National Indian Council on Aging	P.O. Box 2088, Albuquerque, NM 87103	505-242-9505
National Pacific/Asian Resource Center on Aging	2033 6th Avenue, Suite 410, Seattle, WA 98121	206-448-0313
Older Women's League	666 11th Street NW, Lower Level B, Washington, DC 20005	202-783-6686
Pension Rights Center	918 16th Street NW, Suite 704, Washington, DC 20006	202-296-3776
Society for the Right to Die	250 W. 57th Street, New York, NY 10107	212-246-6973
Villers Foundation	1334 G Street NW, Washington, DC 20005	202-628-3030

APPENDIX 16:
DIRECTORY OF NATIONAL LEGAL SERVICES FOR THE ELDERLY

NAME	ADDRESS	TELEPHONE NUMBER
American Bar Association Commission on Legal Problems of the Elderly	1800 M Street N.W., Suite 200, Washington, DC 20036	202-331-2297
Center for Social Gerentology	117 No. 1st Street, Suite 204, Ann Arbor, MI 48104	313-665-1126
Legal Counsel for the Elderly	601 E Street N.W., Washington, DC 20049	202-434-2170
Legal Services for the Elderly	132 W. 43rd Street, 3rd Floor, New York, NY 10036	212-595-1340
Medicare Beneficiaries Defense Fund	1460 Broadway, 8th Floor, New York, NY 10036	212-869-3850
National Academy of Elder Law Atorneys	1604 N. Country Club Road, Tucson, AZ 85716	520-881-4005
National Caucus and Center on Black Aged	1424 K Street, NW, Suite 500, Washington, DC 20005	202-637-8400
National Health Law Program	2639 S. La Cienega Blvd., Los Angeles, CA 90034,	213-204-6010
National Health Law Program	2025 M Street N.W., Washington, DC 20036	202-887-5310
National Senior Citizens Law Center	1052 W. 6th Street, 7th Floor, Los Angeles, CA 90017	213-482-3550
National Senior Citizens Law Center	1101 14th Street N.W., Suite 400, Washington, DC 20005	202-887-5280

APPENDIX 17:
STATE STATUTES CONCERNING ELDER ABUSE

STATE	ADULT PROTECTIVE SERVICES	INSTITUTIONAL ABUSE	LONG-TERM CARE OMBUDSMAN PROGRAM
Alabama	Ala. Code §38-9-1 et seq.	N/A	Ala. Code §22-5A-1 et seq.
Alaska	Alaska Stat. §47.24.010 et seq.	N/A	Alaska Stat. §44.21.231 et seq.
Arizona	Ariz. Rev. Stat. Ann. §46-451 et seq.	N/A	Ariz. Rev. Stat. Ann. §46-452.01 & .02
Arkansas	Ark. Code Ann. §5-28-101 et seq.	N/A	Ark. Code Ann. §20-10-601 et seq.
California	Cal. Welf. & Inst. Code §15750 et seq.	N/A	Cal. Welf. & Inst. Code §9700 et seq.
Colorado	Colo. Rev. Stat. Ann. §26-3.1-101 et seq.	N/A	Colo. Rev. Stat. Ann. §26-11.5-101 et seq.
Connecticut	Conn. Gen. Stat. Ann. §17b-450 et seq.	N/A	Conn. Gen. Stat. Ann. §17b-400 et seq.
Delaware	Del. Code Ann. tit. 31 §3901 et seq.	Del. Code Ann. tit. 16 §1131 et seq.	Del. Code Ann. tit. 16 §1150 et seq.
District of Columbia	D.C. Code Ann. §6-2501 et seq.	N/A	D.C. Code Ann. §6-3501

STATE	ADULT PROTECTIVE SERVICES	INSTITUTIONAL ABUSE	LONG-TERM CARE OMBUDSMAN PROGRAM
Florida	Fla. Stat. Ann. §415.101 et seq.	N/A	Fla. Stat. Ann. §400.0060 et seq.
Georgia	Ga. Code Ann. §30-5-1 et seq.	Ga. Code Ann. §31-8-80 et seq.	Ga. Code Ann. §31-8-51 et seq.
Hawaii	Haw. Rev. Stat. §346-221 et seq.	N/A	Haw. Rev. Stat. §349-12 et seq.
Idaho	Idaho Code §39-5301 et seq.	N/A	Idaho Code §67-5009 et seq.
Illinois	320 Ill. Comp. Stat. 20/1 et seq.	210 Ill. Comp. Stat. 30/1 et seq.	20 Ill. Comp. Stat. 105/4.04
Indiana	Ind. Code Ann. §12-10-3-1 et seq.	N/A	Ind. Code Ann. §12-10-13 et seq.
Iowa	Iowa Code Ann. §235B.1 et seq.	N/A	Iowa Code Ann. §231.41 et seq.
Kansas	Kan. Stat. Ann. §39-1430 et seq.	Kan. Stat. Ann. §39-1401 et seq.	Kan. Stat. Ann. §75-5916 et seq.
Kentucky	Ky. Rev. Stat. Ann. §209.005 et seq.	N/A	Ky. Rev. Stat. Ann. §216.541
Louisiana	La. Rev. Stat. Ann. §14:403.2 et seq.	N/A	La. Rev. Stat. Ann. §40:2010.1 et seq.
Maine	Me. Rev. Stat. Ann. tit. 22 §3470 et seq.	N/A	Me. Rev. Stat. Ann. tit. 22 §5107-A et seq.
Maryland	Md. Code Ann. Fam. Law §14-101 et seq.	Md. Code Ann. Health §19-347	Md. Code Ann. Art. 70B §5
Massachusetts	Mass. Gen. Laws Ann. ch. 19A §14 et seq.	Mass. Gen. Laws Ann. ch. 111 §72F et seq.	Mass. Gen. Laws Ann. ch 19A §27 et seq.
Michigan	Mich. Comp. Laws Ann. §400.11 et seq.	Mich. Comp. Laws Ann. §400.11f	Mich. Comp. Laws Ann. §400.586g et seq.
Minnesota	Minn. Stat. Ann. §626.557 et seq.	N/A	Minn. Stat. Ann. §256.974 et seq.
Mississippi	Miss. Code Ann. §43-47-1 et seq.	Miss. Code Ann. §43-47-37	Miss. Code Ann. §43-7-51 et seq.

STATE	ADULT PROTECTIVE SERVICES	INSTITUTIONAL ABUSE	LONG-TERM CARE OMBUDSMAN PROGRAM
Missouri	Mo. Ann. Stat. §660.250 et seq. & §660.300 et seq.	Mo. Ann. Stat. §198.070	Mo. Ann. Stat. §660.600 et seq.
Montana	Mont. Code Ann. §52-3-801 et seq.	N/A	Mont. Code Ann. §52-3-601 et seq.
Nebraska	Neb. Rev. Stat. §28-348 et seq.	N/A	Neb. Rev. Stat. §81-2237 et seq.
Nevada	Nev. Rev. Stat. Ann. §200.5091 et seq.	N/A	Nev. Rev. Stat. Ann. §427A.125 et seq.
New Hampshire	N.H. Rev. Stat. Ann. §161-F:42 et seq.	N/A	N.H. Rev. Stat. Ann. §161-F:10 et seq.
New Jersey	N.J. Stat. Ann. §52:27D-406 et seq.	N.J. Stat. Ann. §52:27G-7.1	N.J. Stat. Ann. §52:27G-1 et seq.
New Mexico	N.M. Stat. Ann. §27-7-14 et seq.	N/A	N.M. Stat. Ann. §28-17-1 et seq.
New York	N.Y. Soc. Serv. Law Art. 9B §473 et seq.	N/A	N.Y. Exec. Law Art. 19J §544-a et seq.
North Carolina	N.C. Gen. Stat. §108A-99 et seq.	N/A	N.C. Gen. Stat. §143B-181.15 et seq.
North Dakota	N.D. Cent. Code §50-25.2 et seq.	N/A	N.D. Cent. Code §50-10.1-01 et seq.
Ohio	Ohio Rev. Code Ann. §5101.60 et seq.	N/A	Ohio Rev. Code Ann. §173.14 et seq.
Oklahoma	Okla. Stat. Ann. tit. 43A §10-101 et seq.	N/A	Okla. Stat. Ann. tit. 63§1-2211 et seq.
Oregon	Or. Rev. Stat. §124.050 et seq.	Or. Rev. Stat. §441.630 et seq.	Or. Rev. Stat. §441.100 et seq.
Pennsylvania	35 Pa. Cons. Stat. Ann. §10225.101 et seq.	N/A	71 Pa. Cons. Stat. Ann. §581-3 (24.2)
Rhode Island	R.I. Gen. Laws §42-66-4.1 et seq.	R.I. Gen. Laws §23-17.8-1 et seq.	R.I. Gen. Laws §42-66.7-1 et seq.
South Carolina	S.C. Code Ann. §43-35-5 et seq.	N/A	S.C. Code Ann. §43-38-10 et seq.
South Dakota	S.D. Codified Laws Ann. §22-46-1 et seq.	N/A	S.D. Codified Laws Ann. §28-1-45.6 et seq.
Tennessee	Tenn. Code Ann. §71-6-101 et seq.	N/A	Tenn. Code Ann. §71-2-111

STATE	ADULT PROTECTIVE SERVICES	INSTITUTIONAL ABUSE	LONG-TERM CARE OMBUDSMAN PROGRAM
Texas	Tex. Hum. Res. Code Ann. §48.001 et seq.	Tex. Health & Safety Code Ann. §242.121. et seq.	Tex. Hum. Res. Code Ann. §101.051 et seq.
Utah	Utah Code Ann. §62A-3-301 et seq.	N/A	Utah Code Ann. §62A-3-201 et seq.
Vermont	Vt. Stat. Ann. tit. 33 §6901 et seq.	N/A	Vt. Stat. Ann. tit. 33 §7501 et seq.
Virginia	Va. Code Ann. §63.1-55.2 et seq.	N/A	Va. Code Ann. §2.1-373.1 et seq.
Washington	Wash. Rev. Code Ann. §74.34.010 et seq.	N/A	Wash. Rev. Code Ann. §43.190.010 et seq.
West Virginia	W.Va. Code §9-6-1 et seq.	N/A	W.Va. Code §16-5L-1
Wisconsin	Wis. Stat. Ann. §46.90 et seq. & §55.001 et seq.	N/A	Wis. Stat. Ann. §16.009 et seq.
Wyoming	Wyo. Stat. Ann. §35-20-102 et seq.	N/A	Wyo. Stat. Ann. §9-2-1301 et seq.

APPENDIX 18:
RESOURCE DIRECTORY FOR WOMEN VICTIMS OF VIOLENCE

NAME	ADDRESS	TELEPHONE NUMBER
ACTION 1100	Vermont Avenue N.W., Washington, DC 20525	202-934-9396
Black, Indian, Hispanic and Asian Women in Action	122 West Franklin Avenue, Suite 306, Minneapolis, MN 55404	612-870-1193
Center for the Prevention of Sexual and Domestic Violence	1914 North 34th Street, Suite 105, Seattle, WA 98103	800-562-6025
Center for Women Policy Studies	2000 P Street N.W., Suite 508, Washington, DC 20036	202-872-1770
EMERGE	280 Green Street, 2nd Floor, Cambridge, MA 02139	617-547-9870
National Center for Women and Family Law	799 Broadway, Room 402, New York, NY 10003	212-674-8200
National Coalition Against Sexual Assault	2428 Ontario Road N.W., Washington, DC 20009	202-483-7165
National Council on Jewish Women	53 West 23rd Street, New York, NY 10010	212-645-4048
National Organization for Women (NOW)	1000 16th Street N.W., Suite 700, Washington, DC 20036	202-331-0066
Women Against Abuse	P.O. Box 13758, Philadelphia, PA 19101	215-386-1280
Womens Legal Defense Fund	2000 P Street N.W., Suite 400, Washington, DC 20036	202-887-0364

APPENDIX 19:
DIRECTORY OF STATE DOMESTIC VIOLENCE COALITIONS

STATE	DEPARTMENT	ADDRESS	TELEPHONE	FAX
ALABAMA	Alabama Coalition Against Domestic Violence	P.O. Box 4762, Montgomery, AL 36101	334-832-4842	334-832-4803
ALASKA	Alaska Network on Domestic Violence and Sexual Assault	130 Seward Street, Room 501, Juneau, AK 99801	907-586-3650	907-463-4493
ARIZONA	Arizona Coalition Against Domestic Violence	100 West Camelback Street, Suite 109, Phoenix, AZ 85013	602-279-2900	602-279-2980
ARKANSAS	Arkansas Coalition Against Domestic Violence	#1 Sheriff Lane, Suite C, Little Rock, AR 72114	501-812-0571	501-812-0578
CALIFORNIA	California Alliance Against Domestic Violence	926 J Street, Suite 1000, Sacramento, CA 95814	916-444-7163	916-444-7165

STATE	DEPARTMENT	ADDRESS	TELEPHONE	FAX
COLORADO	Colorado Domestic Violence Coalition	P.O. Box 18902, Denver, CO 80218	303-831-9632	303-832-7067
CONNECTICUT	Connecticut Coalition Against Domestic Violence	135 Broad Street, Hartford, CT 06105	860-524-5890	860-249-1408
DISTRICT OF COLUMBIA	D.C. Coalition Against Domestic Violence	P.O. Box 76069, Washington, DC 20013	202-783-5332	202-387-5684
DELAWARE	Delaware Coalition Against Domestic Violence	P.O. Box 847, Wilmington, DE 19899	302-658-2958	302-658-5049
GEORGIA	Georgia Advocates for Battered Women and Children	250 Georgia Avenue SE, Suite 308, Atlanta, GA 30312	404-524-3847	404-524-5959
HAWAII	Hawaii State Coalition Against Domestic Violence	98-939 Moanalua Road, Aiea, HI 96701-5012	808-486-5072	808-486-5169
IDAHO	Idaho Coalition Against Sexual and Domestic Violence	815 Park Blvd., Suite 140, Boise, ID 83712	208-384-0419	208-331-0687
ILLINOIS	Illinois Coalition Against Domestic Violence	730 East Vine Street, Suite 109, Springfield, Illinios 62703	217-789-2830	217-789-1939
INDIANA	Indiana Coalition Against Domestic Violence	2511 E. 46th Street, Suite N-3, Indianapolis, IN 46205	317-543-3908	317-568-4045
IOWA	Iowa Coalition Against Domestic Violence	2603 Bell Avenue, Suite 100, Des Moines, IA 50321	515-244-8028	515-244-7417
KANSAS	Kansas Coalition Against Sexual and Domestic Violence	820 SE Quincy, Suite 422, Topeka, KS 66612	785-232-9784	785-232-9937

STATE	DEPARTMENT	ADDRESS	TELEPHONE	FAX
KENTUCKY	Kentucky Domestic Violence Association	P.O. Box 356, Frankfort, KY 40602	502-875-4132	502-875-4268
LOUISIANA	Louisiana Coalition Against Domestic Violence	P.O. Box 77308, Baton Rouge, LA 70809-7308	504-752-1296	504-751-8927
MAINE	Maine Coalition for Family Crisis Services	128 Main Street, Bangor, ME 04401	207-941-1194	207-941-2327
MARYLAND	Maryland Network Against Domestic Violence	6911 Laurel Bowie Road, Suite 309, Bowie, MD 20715	301-352-4574	301-809-0422
MASSACHUSETTS	Massachusetts Coalition of Battered Women's Service Groups	14 Beacon Street, Suite 507, Boston, MA 02108	617-248-0922	617-248-0902
MICHIGAN	Michigan Coalition Against Domestic Violence and Sexual Assault	913 West Holmes, Suite 211, Lansing, MI 48910	517-887-9334	517-887-9348
MINNESOTA	Minnesota Coalition for Battered Women	450 North Syndicate Street, Suite 122, St. Paul, MN 55104	612-646-1109	612-646-1527
MISSOURI	Missouri Coalition Against Domestic Violence	415 East McCarty, Jefferson City, MO 65101	573-634-4161	573-636-3728
MISSISSIPPI	Mississippi State Coalition Against Domestic Violence	P.O. Box 4703, Jackson, MS 39296-4703	601-981-9196	601-981-2501
MONTANA	Montana Coalition Against Domestic Violence	P.O. Box 633, Helena, MT 59624	406-443-7794	406-443-7818

STATE	DEPARTMENT	ADDRESS	TELEPHONE	FAX
NEBRASKA	Nebraska Domestic Violence and Sexual Assault Coalition	315 South 9th - #18, Lincoln, NE 68508-2253	402-476-6256	n/a
NEVADA	Nevada Network Against Domestic Violence	2100 Capurro Way, Suite E, Sparks, NV 89431	702-358-1171	702-358-0546
NEW HAMPSHIRE	New Hampshire Coalition Against Domestic and Sexual Violence	P.O. Box 353, Concord, NH 03302-0353	603-224-8893	603-228-6096
NEW JERSEY	New Jersey Coalition for Battered Women	2620 Whitehorse/Hamilton Square Road, Trenton, NJ 08690	609-584-8107	609-584-9750
NEW MEXICO	New Mexico State Coalition Against Domestic Violence	P.O. Box 25266, Albuquerque, NM 87125	505-246-9240	505-246-9434
NEW YORK	New York State Coalition Against Domestic Violence	79 Central Avenue, Albany, NY 12206	518-432-4864	518-463-3155
NORTH CAROLINA	North Carolina Coalition Against Domestic Violence	301 West Main Street, Suite 350, Durham, NC 27707	919-956-9124	919-682-1449
NORTH DAKOTA	North Dakota Council on Abused Women's Services	418 East Rosser Avenue, Suite 320, Bismarck, ND 58501	701-255-6240	701-255-1904
OHIO	Ohio Domestic Violence Network	4041 North High Street, Suite 400, Columbus, OH 43214-3247	614-784-0023	614-784-0033

STATE	DEPARTMENT	ADDRESS	TELEPHONE	FAX
OKLAHOMA	Oklahoma Coalition Against Domestic Violence and Sexual Assault	2200 N Classen Blvd., Suite 610, Oklahoma City, OK 73106	405-557-1210	405-557-1296
OREGON	Oregon Coalition Against Domestic and Sexual Violence	520 NW Davis, Suite 310, Portland, OR 97209	503-223-7411	503-223-7490
PENNSYLVANIA	Pennsylvania Coalition Against Domestic Violence	6400 Flank Drive, Suite 1300, Harrisburg, PA 17112-2778	717-545-6400	717-671-8149
RHODE ISLAND	Rhode Island Coalition Against Domestic Violence	422 Post Road, Suite 104, Warwick, RI 02888	401-467-9940	401-467-9943
SOUTH CAROLINA	South Carolina Coalition Against Domestic Violence & Sexual Assault	P.O. Box 7776, Columbia, SC 29202-7776	803-750-1222	803-750-1246
SOUTH DAKOTA	South Dakota Coalition Against Domestic Violence and Sexual Assault	P.O. Box 141, Pierre, SD 57501	605-945-0869	605-945-0870
TENNESSEE	Tennessee Task Force Against Domestic Violence	P.O. Box 120972, Nashville, TN 37212	615-386-9406	615-383-2967
TEXAS	Texas Council on Family Violence	8701 North Mopac Expressway, Suite 450, Austin, TX 78759	512-794-1133	512-794-1199
UTAH	Utah Domestic Violence Advisory Council	120 North 200 West, Suite 425, Salt Lake City, UT 84103	801-538-4100	801-538-3993
VERMONT	Vermont Network Against Domestic Violence and Sexual Assault	P.O. Box 405, Montpelier, VT 05601	802-223-1302	802-2236943

STATE	DEPARTMENT	ADDRESS	TELEPHONE	FAX
VIRGINIA	Virginians Against Domestic Violence	2850 Sandy Bay Road, Suite 101, Williamsburg, VA 23185	.757-221-0990	757-229-1553
WASHINGTON	Washington State Coalition Against Domestic Violence	2101 4th Avenue E, Suite 103, Olympia, WA 98506	360-407-0756	360-352-4078
WEST VIRGINIA	West Virginia Coalition Against Domestic Violence	P.O. Box 85, 181B Main Street, Sutton, WV 26601-0085	304-965-3552	304-765-5071
WISCONSIN	Wisconsin Coalition Against Domestic Violence	1400 East Washington Avenue, Suite 232, Madison, WI 53703-3041	608-255-0539	608-255-3560
WYOMING	Wyoming Coalition Against Domestic Violence and Sexual Assault	P.O. Box 236, Laramie, WY 82073	307-755-5481	307-755-5482
NATIONAL	National Coalition Against Domestic Violence	P.O. Box 18749 Denver, CO 80218	303-839-1852	303-831-9251
NATIONAL	National Coalition Against Domestic Violence Policy Office	119 Constitution Avenue, NE Washington, DC 2002	202-544-7358	202-544-7893

APPENDIX 20:
DIRECTORY OF NATIONAL DOMESTIC VIOLENCE ORGANIZATIONS

NAME	ADDRESS	TELEPHONE	FAX
Family Violence Prevention Fund	383 Rhode Island Street, Suite 304, San Francisco, CA 94103-5133	415-252-8900	415-252-8991
Health Resource Center on Domestic Violence	383 Rhode Island Street, Suite 304, San Francisco, CA 94103-5133	800-313-1310	415-252-8991
National Clearinghouse on Marital and Date Rape	2325 Oak Street, Berkeley, CA 94708	510-524-1582	n/a
National Coalition Against Domestic Violence	P.O. Box 18749, Denver, CO 80218	303-839-1852	303-831-9251
National Coalition Against Domestic Violence Policy Office	119 Constitution Avenue NE, Washington, DC 20002	202-544-7358	202-544-7893
National Network to End Domestic Violence	701 Pennsylvania Avenue NW, Suite 900, Washington, DC 20004	202-347-9520	202-434-7400

NAME	ADDRESS	TELEPHONE	FAX
Battered Women's Justice Project	4032 Chicago Avenue South, Minneapolis, MN 55407	612-824-8768	612-824-8965
Resource Center on Child Custody and Child Protection	P.O. Box 8970, Reno, NV 89507	800-527-3223	702-784-6160
National Resource Center on Domestic Violence	6400 Flank Drive, Suite 1300, Harrisburg, PA 17112	800-537-2238	717-671-8149
National Clearinghouse for the Defense of Battered Women	125 South 9th Street, Suite 302, Philadelphia, PA 19107	800-903-0111	215-351-0779
Battered Women's Justice Project	524 McKnight Street, Reading, PA 19601	800-903-0111	610-373-6403
National Network to End Domestic Violence	8701 North Mopac Expressway, Suite 450, Austin, TX 78759	512-794-1133	512-794-1199
Center for the Prevention of Sexual and Domestic Violence	936 North 34th Street, Suite 200, Seattle, WA 98103	206-634-1903	206-634-0115

APPENDIX 21:
RESOURCE DIRECTORY FOR VICTIMS OF DOMESTIC VIOLENCE

NAME	ADDRESS	TELEPHONE	FAX
Interagency Council Domestic Violence Program	1940 Mesquite Avenue, Lake Havasu City, AZ 86403	520-453-5800	520-453-2787
Southern California Coalition on Battered Women	6308 Woodman Avenue, Suite 117, Van Nuys, CA 91401	818-787-0072	818-787-0073
Delaware Domestic Violence Coordinating Council	900 King Street, Wilmington, DE 19801	302-577-2684	n/a
Georgia Coalition on Family Violence Inc.	1827 Powers Ferry Rd., Bldg 3 - Suite 325, Atlanta, GA 30339	770-984-0085	770-984-0068
Victim's Services Domestic Violence Program	P.O. Box 157, McComb, IL 61455	309-837-6622	309-836-3640
Otter Tail County Intervention Project	Box 815, Fergus Falls, MN 56538	218-739-0983	n/a

NAME	ADDRESS	TELEPHONE	FAX
Missouri Shores Domestic Violence Center	P.O. Box 398, Pierre, SD 57501	605-224-7187	605-244-0256
North Carolina Victim Assistance Network	505 Oberlin Road, Suite 151, Raleigh, NC 27605	919-831-2857	919-831-0824
Long Island Women's Coalition Inc.	P.O. Box 1269M, Bay Shore, NY 11706-0537	516-666-8833	n/a
Action Ohio Coalition for Battered Women	20 South Front Street, Columbus, OH 43215	614-221-1255	614-221-6357
White Buffalo Calf Women's Shelter	P.O. Box 227, Mission, SD 57555	605-856-2317	605-856-2994
Women's Coalition of St. Croix	Box 2734, Christiansted St. Croix, VI 00822	809-773-9272	809-773-9062
Red Cliff Band of Lake Superior Chippewaw Family Violence Program	P.O. Box 529, Bayfield, WI 54814	715-779-3707	715-779-3711

APPENDIX 22:
CALIFORNIA ANTI-STALKING STATUTE

CALIFORNIA PENAL CODE 646.9. STALKING.

(a) Any person who willfully, maliciously, and repeatedly follows or harasses another person and who makes a credible threat with the intent to place that person in reasonable fear for his or her safety, or the safety of his or her immediate family, is guilty of the crime of stalking, punishable by imprisonment in a county jail for not more than one year or by a fine of not more than one thousand dollars ($1,000), or by both that fine and imprisonment, or by imprisonment in the state prison.

(b) Any person who violates subdivision (a) when there is a temporary restraining order, injunction, or any other court order in effect prohibiting the behavior described in subdivision (a) against the same party, shall be punished by imprisonment in the state prison for two, three, or four years.

(c) Every person who, having been convicted of a felony under this section, commits a second or subsequent violation of this section shall be punished by imprisonment in the state prison for two, three, or four years.

(d) In addition to the penalties provided in this section, the sentencing court may order a person convicted of a felony under this section to register as a sex offender pursuant to subparagraph (E) of paragraph (2) of subdivision (a) of Section 290.

(e) For the purposes of this section, "harasses" means a knowing and willful course of conduct directed at a specific person that seriously alarms, annoys, torments, or terrorizes the person, and that serves no legitimate purpose. This course of conduct must be such as would cause a reasonable person to suffer substantial emotional distress, and must actually cause substantial emotional distress to the person.

(f) For purposes of this section, "course of conduct" means a pattern of conduct composed of a series of acts over a period of time, however short, evidencing a continuity of purpose. Constitutionally protected activity is not included within the meaning of "course of conduct."

(g) For the purposes of this section, "credible threat" means a verbal or written threat or a threat implied by a pattern of conduct or a combination of verbal or written statements and conduct made with the intent to place the person that is the target of the threat in reasonable fear for his or her safety or the safety of his or her family and made with the apparent ability to carry out the threat so as to cause the person who is the target of the threat to reasonably fear for his or her safety or the safety of his or her family. It is not necessary to prove that the defendant had the intent to actually carry out the threat. The present incarceration of a person making the threat shall not be a bar to prosecution under this section.

(h) This section shall not apply to conduct that occurs during labor picketing.

(i) If probation is granted, or the execution or imposition of a sentence is suspended, for any person convicted under this section, it shall be a condition of probation that the person participate in counseling, as designated by the court. However, the court, upon a showing of good cause, may find that the counseling requirement shall not be imposed.

(j) The sentencing court also shall consider issuing an order restraining the defendant from any contact with the victim, that may be valid for up to 10 years, as determined by the court. It is the intent of the Legislature that the length of any restraining order be based upon the seriousness of the facts before the court, the probability of future violations, and the safety of the victim and his or her immediate family.

(k) For purposes of this section, "immediate family" means any spouse, parent, child, any person related by consanguinity or affinity within the second degree, or any other person who regularly resides in the household, or who, within the prior six months, regularly resided in the household.

(l) The court shall consider whether the defendant would benefit from treatment pursuant to Section 2684. If it is determined to be appropriate, the court shall recommend that the Department of Corrections make a certification as provided in Section 2684. Upon the certification, the defendant shall be evaluated and transferred to the appropriate hospital for treatment pursuant to Section 2684.

APPENDIX 23:
STATE ANTI-CYBERSTALKING LAWS

STATE	STATUTORY PROVISION
Alabama	Ala. Code § 13A-11-8
Alaska	Alaska Stat. §§ 11.41.260, 11.41.270, 2003 H.B. 12
Arizona	Ariz. Rev. Stat. § 13-2921
Arkansas	Ark. Code § 5-41-108
California	Cal. Civil Code § 1708.7, Cal. Penal Code §§ 422, 646.9, 653m
Colorado	Colo. Rev. Stat. § 18-9-111
Connecticut	Conn. Gen. Stat. § 53a-182b, § 53a-183
Delaware	Del. Code tit. 11 § 1311, tit. 11 § 1312A
Florida	Fla. Stat. § 817.568
Georgia	Code of Georgia § 16-5-90, § 34-1-7
Hawaii	Hawaii Rev. Stat. § 711-1106
Illinois	720 Ill. Comp. Stat. § 5/12-7.5 720 Ill. Comp. Stat. §§ 135/1-2, 135/1-3, 135/2
Indiana	Ind. Code § 35-45-2-2
Iowa	Iowa Code § 708.7
Kansas	Kan. Stat. § 21-3438
Louisiana	La. Rev. Stat. § 14:40.2, La. Rev. Stat. § 14:40.3
Maine	Me. Rev. Stat. tit. 17A § 210-A
Maryland	Md. Code art. 27 § 555C, Md. Code art. 26 § 101
Massachusetts	Mass. Gen. Laws ch. 265 § 43, 43A
Michigan	Mich. Comp. Laws §§ 750.411h, 750.411i, 750.411s
Minnesota	Minn. Stat. § 609.749
Mississippi	Miss. Code § 97-29-45, Miss. Code § 97-45-15 (2003 S.B. 2756)
Missouri	Mo. Rev. Stat. § 565.225

STATE	STATUTORY PROVISION
Montana	Mont. Code § 45-8-213
Nevada	Nev. Rev. Stat. § 200.575
New Hampshire	N.H. Rev. Stat. § 644:4
New Jersey	N.J. Rev. Stat. §§ 2C:33-4, 2C:12-10 (2001 S.B. 1616)
New York	N.Y. Penal Law §§ 215.51, 240.30
North Carolina	N.C. Gen. Stat. §§ 14-196, 14-196.3
North Dakota	N.D. Cent. Code § 12.1-17-07
Ohio	Ohio Code §§ 2913.01(Y), 2917.21(A)
Oklahoma	Okla. Stat. tit. 21 §§ 850, 1173
Oregon	Or. Rev. Stat. §§ 163.730, 166.065
Pennsylvania	Pa. Cons. Stat. tit. 18 § 5504 (1999 Pa. Laws, Act 59) and (2001 Pa. Laws, Act 218)
Rhode Island	R.I. Gen. Laws § 11-52-4.2, § 11-52-4.3
South Carolina	S.C. Code § § 16-3-1700(A)(2), 16-3-1700(B)
South Dakota	S.D. Cod. Laws § 22-19A-1
Tennessee	Tenn. Code § 39-17-308
Texas	Tx. Penal Code 42.07
Vermont	13 V.S.A. §§ 1027, 1061, 1062, 1063
Virginia	Va. Code §§ 18.2-60 18.2-152.7:1
Washington	Wash. Rev. Code §§ 9A.46.020, 9A.46.110, 10.14.020
West Virginia	W. Va. Code §61-3C-14a
Wisconsin	Wis. Stat. § 947.0125
Wyoming	Wyo. Stat. § 6-2-506

Source: National Conference of State Legislatures.

APPENDIX 24:
AVERAGE ANNUAL RATE OF VIOLENT VICTIMIZATION IN THE WORKPLACE, BY OCCUPATION OF VICTIM (1993-1999)

OCCUPATIONAL FIELD	NUMBER	RATE PER 1000 WORKERS	PERCENTAGE OF TOTAL
MEDICAL			
Physician	71,300	16.2	0.6%
Nurse	429,100	21.9	3.5%
Technician	97,600	12.7	0.8%
Other	315,000	8.5	2.6
MENTAL HEALTH			
Professional	290,900	68.2	2.4%
Custodial	60,400	69	0.5%

OCCUPATIONAL FIELD	NUMBER	RATE PER 1000 WORKERS	PERCENTAGE OF TOTAL
Other	186,700	40.7	1.5%
TEACHING			
Preschool	32,900	7.1	0.3%
Elementary	262,700	16.8	2.1%
Junior High	321,300	54.2	2.6%
High School	314,500	38.1	2.6%
College/University	41,600	1.6	0.3%
Technician/Industrial	7,400	12.2	0.1%
Special Education	102,000	68.4	0.8%
Other	169,800	16.7	1.4%
LAW ENFORCEMENT			
Police	1,380,400	260.8	11.2%
Corrections	277,100	155.7	2.3%
Private Security	369,300	86.6	3.0%
Other	359,800	48.3	2.9%
RETAIL SALES			
Convenience Store	336,800	53.9	2.7%
Gas Station	86,900	68.3	0.7%

OCCUPATIONAL FIELD	NUMBER	RATE PER 1000 WORKERS	PERCENTAGE OF TOTAL
Bartender	170,600	81.6	1.4%
Other	1,383,100	15.3	11.2%
TRANSPORTATION			
Bus Driver	105,800	38.2	0.9%
Taxi Cab Driver	84,400	128.3	0.7%
Other	350,500	11.7	2.8%
OTHER OCCUPATIONS	4,720,100	7.0	38.3%

Source: U.S. Department of Justice, Bureau of Justice Statistics.

APPENDIX 25:
DEMOGRAPHIC CHARACTERISTICS OF OFFENDERS COMMITTING WORKPLACE VIOLENCE (1993-1999)

CHARACTERISTIC OF OFFENDER	PERCENT OF VIOLENT VICTIMIZATIONS
Male	82.3%
Female	13%
Male and Female	2%
Gender Unknown	2.7%
White	54.7%
Black	30.2%
Other	9.2%
More than one race	1.8%
Race Unknown	4.0%
Age Under 17	13.5%
Age 18-20	7%
Age 21-29	26.1%
Age 30 or older	43%
Mixed ages	5%
Age Unknown	5.3%
One offender	85.7%
Two offenders	5.9%
Three offenders	2.5%
Four or more offenders	3.3%
Number Unknown	2.6%

Source: U.S. Department of Justice, Bureau of Justice Statistics.

APPENDIX 26:
AVERAGE ANNUAL RATE OF WORKPLACE VICTIMIZATION, BY DEMOGRAPHIC CHARACTERISTICS OF VICTIMS (1993-1999)

CHARACTERISTIC OF VICTIM	RATE PER 1,000 IN WORKFORCE
Male	15
Female	9.6
White	13
Black	10.4
Other	8.2
Hispanic	9.7
Non-Hispanic	12.7
Ethnicity Unknown	19.9
Age 12-19	11.5
Age 20-34	16
Age 25-49	12.3
Age 50-64	7.8
Age 65 or older	3.9
Never Married	14.1
Married	11.3
Widowed	4.7
Divorced/Separated	15.8

Source: U.S. Department of Justice, Bureau of Justice Statistics.

APPENDIX 27:
AVERAGE ANNUAL NUMBER, RATE AND PERCENT OF WORKPLACE VICTIMIZATION, BY TYPE OF CRIME (1993-1999)

CRIME CATEGORY	ANNUAL NUMBER	RATE PER 1000 WORKERS	PERCENT OF WORKPLACE VICTIMIZATION
Homicide	900	0.01	0.1%
Rape/Sexual Assault	36,500	0.3	2.1%
Robbery	70,100	0.5	4.0%
Aggravated Assault	325,000	2.3	18.6%
Simple Assault	1,311,700	9.4	75.2%

Source: U.S. Department of Justice, Bureau of Justice Statistics.

APPENDIX 28:
RESOURCE DIRECTORY FOR VICTIMS OF HATE CRIMES

NAME	ADDRESS	TELEPHONE NUMBER
American Civil Liberties Union	132 West 43rd Street, New York, NY 10036	212-944-9800
American Indian Law Center	P.O. Box 4456, Station A, Albuquerque, NM 87196	505-277-5462
Anti-Defamation League of the B'nai B'rith	823 United Nations Plaza, New York, NY 10017	212-490-2525
Anti-Violence Project, National Gay and Lesbian Task Force	1517 U Street N.W., Washington, DC 20009	202-332-6483
Black, Indian, Hispanic and Asian Women in Action	122 West Franklin Avenue, Suite 306, Minneapolis, MN 55404	612-870-1193
Center for Civil Rights	216 G Street N.E., Washington, DC 20002	202-546-6045
Center for Constitutional Rights (CCR)	666 Broadway, New York, NY 10012	212-614-6464
Center for Democratic Renewal	P.O. Box 50469, Atlanta, GA 30302	404-221-0025
Cultural Survival, Inc.	53-A Church Street, Cambridge, MA 02138	617-495-2562
NAACP Legal Defense Fund	99 Hudson Street, Suite 160, New York, NY 10013	800-221-7822
National Council of Churches	475 Riverside Drive, New York, NY 10027	212-870-2511
National Council on Jewish Women	53 West 23rd Street, New York, NY 10010	212-645-4048

NAME	ADDRESS	TELEPHONE NUMBER
National Indian Justice Center	The McNear Building, 7 Fourth Street, Suite 28, Petaluma, CA 94952	707-762-8113
National Institute Against Prejudice and Violence	31 South Greene Street, Baltimore, MD 21201	301-328-5170
National Organization of Black Law·Enforcement Executives	908 Pennsylvania Avenue S.E., Washington, DC 20003-2227	202-546-8811
National Pacific/Asian Resource Center on Aging	2033 6th Avenue, Suite 410, Seattle, WA 98121	206-448-0313
National Urban League	500 East 62nd Street, New York, NY 10021	800-468-5435
Southern Poverty Law Center	400 Washington Avenue, Montgomery, AL 36104	205-264-2086

APPENDIX 29:
THE HATE CRIMES PREVENTION ACT OF 1999

SECTION 1. SHORT TITLE.

This Act may be cited as the 'Hate Crimes Prevention Act of 1999'.

SECTION 2. FINDINGS.

Congress finds that—

(1) the incidence of violence motivated by the actual or perceived race, color, national origin, religion, sexual orientation, gender, or disability of the victim poses a serious national problem;

(2) such violence disrupts the tranquility and safety of communities and is deeply divisive;

(3) existing Federal law is inadequate to address this problem;

(4) such violence affects interstate commerce in many ways, including—

(A) by impeding the movement of members of targeted groups and forcing such members to move across State lines to escape the incidence or risk of such violence; and

(B) by preventing members of targeted groups from purchasing goods and services, obtaining or sustaining employment or participating in other commercial activity;

(5) perpetrators cross State lines to commit such violence;

(6) instrumentalities of interstate commerce are used to facilitate the commission of such violence;

(7) such violence is committed using articles that have traveled in interstate commerce;

(8) violence motivated by bias that is a relic of slavery can constitute badges and incidents of slavery;

(9) although many State and local authorities are now and will continue to be responsible for prosecuting the overwhelming majority of violent crimes in the United States, including violent crimes motivated by bias, Federal jurisdiction over certain violent crimes motivated by bias is necessary to supplement State and local jurisdiction and ensure that justice is achieved in each case;

(10) Federal jurisdiction over certain violent crimes motivated by bias enables Federal, State, and local authorities to work together as partners in the investigation and prosecution of such crimes; and

(11) the problem of hate crime is sufficiently serious, widespread, and interstate in nature as to warrant Federal assistance to States and local jurisdictions.

SECTION 3. DEFINITION OF HATE CRIME.

In this Act, the term 'hate crime' has the same meaning as in section 280003(a) of the Violent Crime Control and Law Enforcement Act of 1994 (28 U.S.C. 994 note).

SECTION 4. PROHIBITION OF CERTAIN ACTS OF VIOLENCE.

Section 245 of title 18, United States Code, is amended—

(1) by redesignating subsections (c) and (d) as subsections (d) and (e), respectively; and

(2) by inserting after subsection (b) the following:

'(c)(1) Whoever, whether or not acting under color of law, willfully causes bodily injury to any person or, through the use of fire, a firearm, or an explosive device, attempts to cause bodily injury to any person, because of the actual or perceived race, color, religion, or national origin of any person—

(A) shall be imprisoned not more than 10 years, or fined in accordance with this title, or both; and

(B) shall be imprisoned for any term of years or for life, or fined in accordance with this title, or both if—

(i) death results from the acts committed in violation of this paragraph; or

(ii) the acts omitted in violation of this paragraph include kidnapping or an attempt to kidnap, aggravated sexual abuse or an attempt to commit aggravated sexual abuse, or an attempt to kill.

(2)(A) Whoever, whether or not acting under color of law, in any circumstance described in subparagraph (B), willfully causes bodily injury to any person or, through the use of fire, a firearm, or an explosive device, attempts to cause bodily injury to any person, because of the actual or perceived religion, gender, sexual orientation, or disability of any person—

(i) shall be imprisoned not more than 10 years, or fined in accordance with this title, or both; and

(ii) shall be imprisoned for any term of years or for life, or fined in accordance with this title, or both, if—

(I) death results from the acts committed in violation of this paragraph; or

(II) the acts committed in violation of this paragraph include kidnapping or an attempt to kidnap, aggravated sexual abuse or an attempt to commit aggravated sexual abuse, or an attempt to kill.

(B) For purposes of subparagraph (A), the circumstances described in this subparagraph are that—

(i) in connection with the offense, the defendant or the victim travels in interstate or foreign commerce, uses a facility or instrumentality of interstate or foreign commerce, or engages in any activity affecting interstate or foreign commerce; or

(ii) the offense is in or affects interstate or foreign commerce.'.

SECTION 5. DUTIES OF FEDERAL SENTENCING COMMISSION.

(a) AMENDMENT OF FEDERAL SENTENCING GUIDELINES—Pursuant to its authority under section 994 of title 28, United States Code, the United States Sentencing Commission shall study the issue of adult recruitment of juveniles to commit hate crimes and shall, if appropriate, amend the Federal sentencing guidelines to provide sentencing enhancements (in addition to the sentencing enhancement provided for the use of a minor during the commission of an offense) for adult defendants who recruit juveniles to assist in the commission of hate crimes.

(b) CONSISTENCY WITH OTHER GUIDELINES—In carrying out this section, the United States Sentencing Commission shall—

(1) ensure that there is reasonable consistency with other Federal sentencing guidelines; and

(2) avoid duplicative punishments for substantially the same offense.

SECTION 6. GRANT PROGRAM.

(a) AUTHORITY TO MAKE GRANTS—The Office of Justice Programs of the Department of Justice shall make grants, in accordance with such regulations as the Attorney General may prescribe, to State and local programs designed to combat hate crimes committed by juveniles, including programs to train local law enforcement officers in investigating, prosecuting, and preventing hate crimes.

(b) AUTHORIZATION OF APPROPRIATIONS—There are authorized to be appropriated such sums as may be necessary to carry out this section.

SECTION 7. AUTHORIZATION FOR ADDITIONAL PERSONNEL TO ASSIST STATE AND LOCAL LAW ENFORCEMENT.

There are authorized to be appropriated to the Department of the Treasury and the Department of Justice, including the Community Relations Service, for fiscal years 1998, 1999, and 2000 such sums as are necessary to increase the number of personnel to prevent and respond to alleged violations of section 245 of title 18, United States Code (as amended by this Act).

SECTION 8. SEVERABILITY.

If any provision of this Act, an amendment made by this Act, or the application of such provision or amendment to any person or circumstance is held to be unconstitutional, the remainder of this Act, the amendments made by this Act, and the application of the provisions of such to any person or circumstance shall not be affected thereby.

APPENDIX 30:
STATE PSYCHOLOGICAL ASSOCIATIONS

STATE	ADDRESS	TELEPHONE NUMBER
Alabama Psychological Association	P.O. Box 97, Montgomery, AL 36101-0097	205-262-8245
Alaska Psychological Association	P.O. Box 241292, Anchorage, AK 99524	907-696-8921
Arkansas Psychological Association	Three Financial Center, 900 S. Shackleford, Suite 300, Little Rock, AR 72211	501-228-5550
Arizona Psychological Association	6210 E. Thomas Rd., Suite 209, Scottsdale, AZ 85251	602-675-9477
California Psychological Association	1010 Eleventh Street, Suite 202, Sacramento, CA 95814-3807	916-325-9786
Colorado Psychological Association	1660 S. Albion, Suite 712, Denver, CO 80222	303-692-9303
Connecticut Psychological Association	50 Founders Plaza, Suite 107, East Hartford, CT 06108	203-528-8550
District of Columbia Psychological Association	750 First Street N.E., Suite 5127, Washington, DC 20002-4241	202-336-5557
Delaware Psychological Association	P.O. Box 718, Claymont, DE 19703-0718	302-475-1574
Florida Psychological Association	408 Office Plaza, Tallahassee, FL 32301-2757	904-656-2222
Georgia Psychological Association	1800 Peachtree Street N.W., Suite 525, Atlanta, GA 30309	404-351-9555
Hawaii Psychological Association	P.O. Box 10456, Honolulu, HI 96816-0456	808-377-5992

STATE	ADDRESS	TELEPHONE NUMBER
Iowa Psychological Association	P.O. Box 320, Knoxville, IA 50138-0320	515-828-884
Idaho Psychological Association	1365 North Orchard, Suite 316, Boise, ID 83706	208-376-2273
Illinois Psychological Association	203 N. Wabash, Suite 910, Chicago, IL 60601-2413	312-372-7610
Indiana Psychological Association	55 Monument Circle, Suite 700, Indianapolis, IN 46204	317-686-5348
Kansas Psychological Association	400 S.W. Croix, Topeka, KS 66611-2251	913-267-7435
Kentucky Psychological Association	120 Sears Avenue, Suite 202, Louisville, KY 40207-5063	502-894-0777
Louisiana Psychological Association	P.O. Box 66924, Baton Rouge, LA 70896-6924	504-344-8839
Maine Psychological Association	12 Spruce Street, Box 5435, Augusta, ME 04330	207-621-0732
Maryland Psychological Association	1 Mall North, Suite 314, 10025 Governor Warfield Parkway, Columbia, MD 21044	410-992-4258
Massachusetts Psychological Association	14 Beacon Street, Suite 714, Boston, MA 02108-3741	617-523-6320
Michigan Psychological Association	24350 Orchard Lake Rd., Suite 105, Farmington, MI 48336	810-473-9070
Minnesota Psychological Association	1740 Rice Street, Suite 220, St. Paul, MN 55113-6811	612-489-2964
Missouri Psychological Association	410 Madison St., Jefferson City, MO 65101-2989	314-634-8852
Mississippi Psychological Association	P.O. Box 1120, 812 N. President Street, Jackson, MS 39215-1120	601-353-1672
Montana Psychological Association	P.O. Box 6367, Helena, MT 59604-6367	406-227-5292
Nebraska Psychological Association	1044 H Street, Lincoln, NE 68508-3169	402-475-0709
Nevada Psychological Association	3601 Skyline Blvd., Suite 35, Reno, NV 89509	702-827-6944
New Hampshire Psychological Association	P.O. Box 1205, Concord, NH 03301	603-225-9925

STATE	ADDRESS	TELEPHONE NUMBER
New Jersey Psychological Association	349 E. Northfield Road, Suite 211, Livingston, NJ 07039-4806	201-535-9888
New Mexico Psychological Association	2501 San Pedro N.E., Suite 113, Albuquerque, NM 87110	505-883-7376
New York State Psychological Association	Executive Park East, Albany, NY 12203	518-437-1040
North Carolina Psychological Association	1004 Dresser Court, Suite 106, Raleigh, NC 27609-7353	919-872-1005
North Dakota Psychological Association	116 N. 4th St., Suite 130, Bismarck, ND 58501-2486	701-223-9045
Ohio Psychological Association	400 East Town Street, Suite 020, Columbus, OH 43215-1599	614-224-0034
Oklahoma Psychological Association	P.O. Box 18508, 708 N.E. 42nd Street, Oklahoma City, OK 73154-0508	405-424-0019
Oregon Psychological Association	147 N.E. 102nd, Portland, OR 97216	503-253-9155
Pennsylvania Psychological Association	416 Forster Street, Harrisburg, PA 17102-1714	717-232-3817
Rhode Island Psychological Association	Independence Square, 500 Prospect Street, Pawtucket, RI 02860-6260	401-728-5570
South Carolina Psychological Association	P.O. Box 5207, Columbia, SC 29250-5207	803-771-6050
South Dakota Psychological Association	1208 Elkhorn St., Sioux Falls, SD 57104	605-332-3386
Tennessee Psychological Association	530 Church Street, Suite 300, Nashville, TN 37219-2394	615-254-3687
Texas Psychological Association	6633 E. Highway 290, Suite 305, Austin, TX 78723-1158	512-454-2449
Utah Psychological Association	2102 East 3780 South, Salt Lake City, UT 84109	801-278-4665
Virginia Psychological Association	109 Amherst Street, Winchester, VA 22601-4182	703-667-5544
Vermont Psychological Association	P.O. Box 1017, Montpelier, VT 05601-1017	802-229-5447

STATE	ADDRESS	TELEPHONE NUMBER
Washington State Psychological Association	P.O. Box 2016, Edmonds, WA 98020-2016	206-363-9772
West Virginia Psychological Association	P.O. Box 536, Scott Depot, WV 25560	304-757-0458
Wisconsin Psychological Association	121 South Hancock Street, Madison, WI 53703-3461	608-251-1450
Wyoming Psychological Association	P.O. Box 1191, Laramie, WY 82070-1191	307-745-3167

APPENDIX 31:
RESOURCE DIRECTORY OF ORGANIZATIONS WHICH ASSIST CRIME VICTIMS

NAME	ADDRESS	TELEPHONE NUMBER
American Association for Counseling	5999 Stevenson Avenue, Alexandria, VA 22304	703-823-9800
American Bar Association, Victims Committee	1800 M Street N.W., 2nd Floor South, Washington, DC 20036	202-331-2260
American Civil Liberties Union	132 West 43rd Street, New York, NY 10036	212-944-9800
Citizen Action	1300 Connecticut Avenue N.W., Suite 401, Washington, DC 20036	202-857-5153
The Compassionate Friends	P.O. Box 1347, Oak Brook, IL 60521	312-990-0010
Concerns of Police Survivors	P.O. Box 3199, Camdenton, MO 65020	800-784-2677
Family and Friends of Missing Persons and Violent Crime Victims	P.O. Box 27529, Seattle, WA 98125	206-362-1081
Handgun Control	1225 I Street N.W., Washington, DC 20005	202-898-0792
Institute for Victims of Trauma	6801 Market Square Drive, McLean, VA 22101	703-847-8456
National Association of Crime Victim Compensation Boards	P.O. Box 16003, Alexandria, VA 22302	703-370-2996
The National Center for Citizen Involvement	1111 Nineteenth Street, North, Arlington, VA 20005	703-276-0542

NAME	ADDRESS	TELEPHONE NUMBER
National Crime Prevention Council	1700 K Street N.W., 2nd Floor, Washington, DC 20006	202-466-6272
National Criminal Justice Association	444 North Capitol Street N.W., Washington, DC 20001	202-347-4900
National Organization for Victim Assistance (NOVA)	1757 Park Road N.W., Washington, DC 20010	202-232-6682
National Victim Center	307 West Seventh Street, Suite 1001, Fort Worth, TX 76102	817-877-3855
No Greater Love	1750 New York Avenue N.W., Washington, DC 20006	202-783-4665
Office for Victims of Crime, U.S. Department of Justice	633 Indiana Avenue N.W., 13th Floor, Washington, DC 20531	202-724-5947
The Society for Traumatic Stress Studies	P.O. Box 1564, Lancaster, PA 17603	717-396-8877
They Help Each Other Spiritually National Headquarters	410 Penn Hills Mall, Pittsburgh, PA 15235	412-471-7779
Trial Lawyers for Public Justice	1625 Massachusetts Avenue N.W., Suite 100, Washington, DC 20036	202-797-8600
U.S. Association for Victim/Offender Mediation	254 South Morgan Boulevard, Valparaiso, IN 46383	219-462-1127

APPENDIX 32:
STATE VICTIM COMPENSATION PROGRAMS

STATE	ADDRESS	TELEPHONE NUMBER
Alabama Crime Victims Compensation Commission	P.O. Box 1548, Montgomery, AL 36102	205-242-4007
Alaska Violent Crime Compensation Board	P.O. Box 111200, Juneau, AK 99811	907-465-3040
Arizona Criminal Justice Commission	1501 West Washington, Suite 207, Phoenix, AZ 85007	602-542-1928
Arkansas Crime Victims Reparations Board	601 Tower Building, 323 Center Street, Little Rock, AR 72201	501-682-1323
California Victims of Crime Program	P.O. Box 3036, Sacramento, CA 95812	916-323-6251
Colorado Division of Criminal Justice	700 Kipling Street, Suite 3000, Denver, CO 80215	303-271-6840
Connecticut Commission on Victim Services	1155 Silas Deane Highway, Wethersfield, CT 06109	203-529-3089
Delaware Violent Crime Compensation Board	1500 East Newport Pike, Suite 10, Wilmington, DE 19804	302-995-8383
District of Columbia Crime Victims Compensation Program	1200 Upshur Street N.W., Washington, DC 20011	202-576-7706
Florida Division of Victim Services	The Capitol PL-01, Tallahassee, FL 32399	904-488-0848
Georgia Crime Victim Compensation Program	503 Oak Place South, Suite 540, Atlanta, GA 30349	404-559-4949

STATE	ADDRESS	TELEPHONE NUMBER
Hawaii Criminal Injuries Compensation Commission	335 Merchant Street, Suite 244, Honolulu, HI 96813	808-587-1143
Idaho Victim Compensation Program	317 Main Street, Boise, ID 83720	208-334-6000
Illinois Crime Victims Division	100 W. Randolf, 13th Floor, Chicago, IL 60601	312-814-2581
Indiana Violent Crimes Victim Compensation Division	402 W. Washington Street, Room W-382, Indianapolis, IN 46204	317-232-3809
Iowa Crime Victim Assistance Program	Old Historical Building, Des Moines, IA 50319	515-281-5044
Kansas Crime Victims Reparations Board	700 S.W. Jackson, Suite 400, Topeka, KS 66603	913-296-2359
Kentucky Crime Victims Compensation Board	115 Myrtle Avenue, Frankfort, KY 40601	502-564-2290
Louisiana Crime Victims Reparations Board	1885 Wooddale Boulevard, Suite 708, Baton Rouge, LA 70806	504-925-4437
Maine Crime Victim Compensation Program	State House Station #6, Augusta, ME 04333	207-626-8589
Maryland Criminal Injuries Compensation Board	6776 Reisterstown Road, Suite 313, Baltimore, MD 21215	410-764-4214
Massachusetts Victims Compensation and Assistance	One Ashburton Place, Boston, MA 02108	617-727-2300
Michigan Crime Victims Compensation Board	P.O. Box 30026, Lansing, MI 48909	517-373-7373
Minnesota Crime Victims Reparations Board	1821 University Avenue, Suite N465, St. Paul, MN 55104	612-642-0395
Mississippi Crime Victim Compensation Program	P.O. Box 267, Jackson, MS 39205	800-829-6766
Missouri Crime Victims Compensation Unit	P.O. Box 58, Jefferson City, MO 65102	314-525-6006
Montana Crime Victims Unit	303 North Roberts, 4th Floor, Helena, MT 59620	406-444-3653
Nebraska Commission on Law Enforcement	P.O. Box 94946, Lincoln, NE 68509	402-471-2828

STATE	ADDRESS	TELEPHONE NUMBER
Nevada Victims of Crime Program	2770 Maryland Parkway, Suite 416, Las Vegas, NV 89109	702-486-7259
New Hampshire Victims Compensation Program	State House Annex, Concord, NH 03301	603-271-1284
New Jersey Violent Crimes Compensation Board	60 Park Place, Suite 10, Newark, NJ 07102	201-648-2107
New Mexico Crime Victims Reparations Commission	8100 Mountain Road N.E., Suite 106, Albuquerque, NM 87110	505-841-9432
New York Crime Victims Board	270 Broadway, Room 200, New York, NY 10007	212-417-5133
North Carolina Victim and Justice Services	P.O. Box 27687, Raleigh, NC 27611	919-733-7974
North Dakota Crime Victims Reparations Program	P.O. Box 5521, Bismarck, ND 58502	701-221-6195
Ohio Victims of Crime Compensation Program	65 East State Street, Suite 1100, Columbus, OH 43215	614-466-7190
Oklahoma Crime Victims Compensation Board	2200 Classen Boulevard, Suite 1800 Oklahoma City, OK 73106	405-557-6704
Oregon Crime Victims Assistance Section	Department of Justice, 100 Justice Building, Salem, OR 97310	503-378-5348
Pennsylvania Crime Victims Compensation Board	333 Market Street, Lobby Level, Harrisburg, PA 17191	717-783-5153
Rhode Island Judicial Planning Section, Supreme Court	250 Benefit Street, Providence, RI 02903	401-227-2500
South Carolina Division of Victim Assistance	P.O. Box 210009, Columbia, SC 29221	803-737-8142
South Dakota Crime Victims Compensation Commission	115 East Dakota Avenue, Pierre, SD 57501	605-773-3478
Tennessee Division of Claims Administration	Andrew Jackson Building, 11th Floor, Volunteer Plaza, Nashville, TN 37243	615-741-2734

STATE	ADDRESS	TELEPHONE NUMBER
Texas Crime Victim Compensations Division	P.O. Box 12548, Capitol Station, Austin, TX 78711	512-462-6400
Utah Office of Crime Victim Reparations	350 East 500 South, Suite 200, Salt Lake City, UT 84111	801-533-4000
Vermont Center for Crime Victim Services	P.O. Box 991, Montpelier, VT 05601	802-828-3374
Virginia Crime Victims Compensation Division	P.O. Box 5423, Richmond, VA 23220	804-367-8686
Washington Crime Victim Compensation Program	P.O. Box 44520, Olympia, WA 98504	206-956-5340
West Virginia Crime Victim Compensation	1900 Kanawha Boulevard East, Building 1, Room 6, Charleston, WV 25305	304-558-3471
Wisconsin Office of Crime Victim Services	P.O. Box 7951, Madison, WI 53707	608-266-6470
Wyoming Crime Victims Compensation Commission	1700 Westland Road, Cheyenne, WY 82002	307-635-4050

APPENDIX 33:
ELIGIBLE PERSONS UNDER STATE VICTIM COMPENSATION PROGRAMS

STATE	ELIGIBLE PERSONS
Alabama	Injured party, spouse, children, parents and siblings
Alaska	Injured party, spouse, children, parents and siblings
Arizona	Injured party, spouse, children, parents and siblings
Arkansas	Injured party, spouse, children, parents and siblings
California	Injured party, spouse, children, parents and siblings
Colorado	Injured party, families and secondary victims
Connecticut	Injured party, spouse, children, parents and siblings
Delaware	Injured party, spouse, children, parents and siblings
District of Columbia	Injured party, spouse, children, and parents of victim when victim is killed
Florida	Injured party, spouse, children, parents and siblings
Georgia	Injured party, spouse, children, parents, guardian and "Good Samaritans"
Hawaii	Injured party, spouse, children, parents and siblings
Idaho	Injured party, spouse, children, parents and siblings
Illinois	Injured party
Indiana	Injured party, spouse, children, parents and siblings
Iowa	Injured party, spouse, children, parents and siblings
Kansas	Injured party, spouse, children and parents
Kentucky	Injured party, spouse, children, parents and siblings
Louisiana	Injured party, spouse, children and parents
Maine	Injured party
Maryland	Injured party, spouse, children, parents and siblings
Massachusetts	Injured party, spouse, children, parents and siblings

STATE	ELIGIBLE PERSONS
Michigan	Injured party, spouse, children, parents and siblings
Minnesota	Injured party, spouse, children, parents and siblings
Mississippi	Injured party, spouse and children
Missouri	Injured party, spouse, children, parents and siblings
Montana	Injured party, spouse, children, parents and siblings
Nebraska	Injured party, spouse, children, parents and siblings
Nevada	Injured party, spouse, children and parents
New Hampshire	Injured party, spouse, children and parents
New Jersey	Injured party, spouse, children, parents and siblings
New Mexico	Injured party, spouse, children, parents and siblings
New York	Injured party, spouse, children, parents and siblings
North Carolina	Injured party, spouse, children, parents and siblings
North Dakota	Injured party
Ohio	Injured party, dependent of deceased victim, someone who has paid the expenses of the victim and "Good Samaritans"
Oklahoma	Injured party, spouse, children, parents and siblings
Oregon	Injured party, spouse, children, parents and siblings
Pennsylvania	Injured party, spouse, children, parents and siblings
Rhode Island	Injured party, spouse, children, parents and siblings
South Carolina	Injured party, spouse, children, parents and siblings
South Dakota	Injured party, spouse, children, parents and "Good Samaritans"
Tennessee	Injured party, spouse, children, parents and siblings
Texas	Injured party, spouse, children, parents and siblings
Utah	Injured party, spouse, children, parents and siblings
Vermont	Injured party and dependents
Virginia	Injured party, spouse, children, parents and siblings
Washington	Injured party, spouse, children, parents and siblings
West Virginia	Injured party, spouse, children, parents and siblings
Wisconsin	Injured party, spouse, children, parents and siblings
Wyoming	Injured party, spouse, children, parents and siblings

APPENDIX 34:
COMPENSABLE CRIMES UNDER STATE VICTIM COMPENSATION PROGRAMS

STATE	COMPENSABLE CRIMES
Alabama	Assault and battery, child physical and/or sexual abuse, domestic abuse, drunk driving, homicide, motor vehicle crime, rape, robbery, sex offenses and spousal abuse
Alaska	Assault and battery, child physical and/or sexual abuse, domestic abuse, drunk driving, homicide, motor vehicle crime, rape, robbery, sex offenses and spousal abuse
Arizona	Assault and battery, child physical and/or sexual abuse, domestic abuse, drunk driving, homicide, rape, robbery, sex offenses and spousal abuse
Arkansas	Assault and battery, child physical and/or sexual abuse, domestic abuse, drunk driving, homicide, motor vehicle crime, rape, robbery, sex offenses and spousal abuse
California	Assault and battery, child physical and/or sexual abuse, domestic abuse, drunk driving, homicide, motor vehicle crime, rape, robbery, sex offenses and spousal abuse
Colorado	Assault and battery, child physical and/or sexual abuse, domestic abuse, drunk driving, homicide, motor vehicle crime, rape, robbery, sex offenses and spousal abuse
Connecticut	Assault and battery, child physical and/or sexual abuse, domestic abuse, drunk driving, homicide, motor vehicle crime, rape, robbery, sex offenses and spousal abuse
Delaware	Assault and battery, child physical and/or sexual abuse, domestic abuse, drunk driving, homicide, motor vehicle crime, rape, robbery, sex offenses and spousal abuse
District of Columbia	Assault and battery, child physical and/or sexual abuse, domestic abuse, drunk driving, homicide, motor vehicle crime, rape, robbery, sex offenses and spousal abuse
Florida	Assault and battery, child physical and/or sexual abuse, drunk driving, homicide, rape, robbery, sex offenses

STATE	COMPENSABLE CRIMES
Georgia	Assault and battery, child physical and/or sexual abuse, domestic abuse, homicide, motor vehicle crime
Hawaii	Assault and battery, child physical and/or sexual abuse, domestic abuse, homicide, motor vehicle crime, rape, robbery and sex offenses
Idaho	Assault and battery, child physical and/or sexual abuse, domestic abuse, drunk driving, homicide, motor vehicle crime, rape, robbery, sex offenses and spousal abuse
Illinois	Assault and battery, child physical and/or sexual abuse, domestic abuse, drunk driving, homicide, rape, sex offenses and spousal abuse
Indiana	Assault and battery, child physical and/or sexual abuse, domestic abuse, drunk driving, homicide, motor vehicle crime, rape, robbery, sex offenses and spousal abuse
Iowa	Assault and battery, child physical and/or sexual abuse, domestic abuse, drunk driving, homicide, motor vehicle crime, rape, robbery, sex offenses and spousal abuse
Kansas	Assault and battery, child physical and/or sexual abuse, domestic abuse, drunk driving, homicide, rape, sex offenses and spousal abuse
Kentucky	Assault and battery, child physical and/or sexual abuse, drunk driving, homicide, rape and sex offenses
Louisiana	Assault and battery, child physical and/or sexual abuse, domestic abuse, homicide, motor vehicle crime, rape, robbery, sex offenses and spousal abuse
Maine	Assault and battery, child physical and/or sexual abuse, domestic abuse, drunk driving, homicide, motor vehicle crime, robbery and sex offenses
Maryland	Assault and battery, child physical and/or sexual abuse, domestic abuse, drunk driving, homicide, motor vehicle crime, rape, sex offenses and spousal abuse
Massachusetts	Assault and battery, child physical and/or sexual abuse, domestic abuse, drunk driving, homicide, motor vehicle crime, rape, robbery, sex offenses and spousal abuse
Michigan	Assault and battery, child physical and/or sexual abuse, domestic abuse, drunk driving, homicide, motor vehicle crime, rape, robbery, sex offenses and spousal abuse
Minnesota	Assault and battery, child physical and/or sexual abuse, domestic abuse, drunk driving, homicide, rape, robbery, sex offenses and spousal abuse
Mississippi	Assault and battery, child physical and/or sexual abuse, domestic abuse, drunk driving, homicide, motor vehicle crime, rape, robbery, sex offenses and spousal abuse

STATE	COMPENSABLE CRIMES
Missouri	Assault and battery, child physical and/or sexual abuse, domestic abuse, drunk driving, homicide, motor vehicle crime, rape, sex offenses and spousal abuse
Montana	Assault and battery, child physical and/or sexual abuse, domestic abuse, homicide, rape, robbery, sex offenses and spousal abuse
Nebraska	Assault and battery, child physical and/or sexual abuse, domestic abuse, drunk driving, homicide, rape, sex offenses and spousal abuse
Nevada	Assault and battery, child physical and/or sexual abuse, domestic abuse, drunk driving, homicide, rape, robbery, sex offenses and spousal abuse
New Hampshire	Assault and battery, child physical and/or sexual abuse, domestic abuse, drunk driving, homicide, motor vehicle crime, rape, robbery, sex offenses and spousal abuse
New Jersey	Assault and battery, child physical and/or sexual abuse, domestic abuse, homicide, rape, robbery, sex offenses and spousal abuse
New Mexico	Assault and battery, child sexual abuse, drunk driving, homicide, motor vehicle crime and rape
New York	Assault and battery, child physical and/or sexual abuse, domestic abuse, drunk driving, homicide, motor vehicle crime, rape, robbery, sex offenses and spousal abuse
North Carolina	Assault and battery, child physical and/or sexual abuse, domestic abuse, homicide, motor vehicle crime, rape, robbery, sex offenses and spousal abuse
North Dakota	Assault and battery, child physical and/or sexual abuse, domestic abuse, drunk driving, homicide, rape, robbery, sex offenses and spousal abuse
Ohio	Assault and battery, child physical and/or sexual abuse, domestic abuse, homicide, motor vehicle crime, rape, robbery, sex offenses and spousal abuse
Oklahoma	Assault and battery, child physical and/or sexual abuse, domestic abuse, homicide, motor vehicle crime, rape, robbery, sex offenses and spousal abuse
Oregon	Assault and battery, child physical and/or sexual abuse, domestic abuse, drunk driving, homicide, motor vehicle crime, rape, robbery, sex offenses and spousal abuse
Pennsylvania	Assault and battery, child physical and/or sexual abuse, domestic abuse, homicide, rape, robbery, sex offenses and spousal abuse
Rhode Island	Assault and battery, child physical and/or sexual abuse, domestic abuse, drunk driving, homicide, motor vehicle crime, rape, robbery, sex offenses and spousal abuse

STATE	COMPENSABLE CRIMES
South Carolina	Assault and battery, child physical and/or sexual abuse, domestic abuse, drunk driving, homicide, motor vehicle crime, rape and sex offenses
South Dakota	Assault and battery, child physical and/or sexual abuse, domestic abuse, drunk driving, homicide, motor vehicle crime, rape, robbery, sex offenses and spousal abuse
Tennessee	Assault and battery, child physical and/or sexual abuse, domestic abuse, drunk driving, homicide, rape, robbery, sex offenses and spousal abuse
Texas	Assault and battery, child physical and/or sexual abuse, domestic abuse, drunk driving, homicide, motor vehicle crime, rape, robbery, sex offenses and spousal abuse
Utah	Assault and battery, child physical and/or sexual abuse, domestic abuse, drunk driving, homicide, motor vehicle crime, rape, robbery, sex offenses and spousal abuse
Vermont	Assault and battery, child sexual abuse, domestic abuse, drunk driving, homicide and sex offenses
Virginia	Assault and battery, child physical and/or sexual abuse, domestic abuse, drunk driving, homicide, rape, robbery, sex offenses and spousal abuse
Washington	Assault and battery, child physical and/or sexual abuse, domestic abuse, drunk driving, homicide, motor vehicle crime, rape, robbery, sex offenses and spousal abuse
West Virginia	Assault and battery, child physical and/or sexual abuse, domestic abuse, drunk driving, homicide, motor vehicle crime, rape, robbery, sex offenses and spousal abuse
Wisconsin	Assault and battery, child physical and/or sexual abuse, domestic abuse, drunk driving, homicide, motor vehicle crime, rape, robbery, sex offenses and spousal abuse
Wyoming	Assault and battery, child physical and/or sexual abuse, domestic abuse, drunk driving, homicide, rape, robbery, sex offenses and spousal abuse

APPENDIX 35:
MAXIMUM COMPENSATION AVAILABLE UNDER STATE VICTIM COMPENSATION STATUTES

STATE	MAXIMUM AWARD OF COMPENSATION
Alabama	$10,000
Alaska	$40,000
Arizona	$10,000
Arkansas	$10,000
California	$6,000
Colorado	$10,000
Connecticut	$25,000
Delaware	$25,000
District of Columbia	$25,000
Florida	$10,000
Georgia	$1,000
Hawaii	$10,000
Idaho	$25,000
Illinois	$25,000
Indiana	$10,000
Iowa	$20,600
Kansas	$10,000
Kentucky	$25,000
Louisiana	$10,000
Maine	$5,000
Maryland	$45,000
Massachusetts	$25,000

STATE	MAXIMUM AWARD OF COMPENSATION
Michigan	$25,000
Minnesota	$50,000
Mississippi	$10,000
Missouri	$10,000
Montana	$25,000
Nebraska	$10,000
Nevada	$15,000
New Hampshire	$5,000
New Jersey	$25,000
New Mexico	$12,500
New York	unlimited
North Carolina	$22,000
North Dakota	$25,000
Ohio	$50,000
Oklahoma	$10,000
Oregon	$23,000
Pennsylvania	$35,000
Rhode Island	$25,000
South Carolina	$10,000
South Dakota	$10,000
Tennessee	$5,000
Texas	$25,000
Utah	$50,000
Vermont	$10,000
Virginia	$15,000
Washington	$20,000
West Virginia	$50,000
Wisconsin	$40,000
Wyoming	$10,000

GLOSSARY

Abduction—The criminal or tortious act of taking and carrying away by force.

Accusation—An indictment, presentment, information or any other form in which a charge of a crime or offense can be made against an individual.

Accusatory Instrument—The initial pleading which forms the procedural basis for a criminal charge, such as an indictment.

Accuse—To directly and formally institute legal proceedings against a person, charging that he or she has committed an offense.

Acquit—A verdict of "not guilty" which determines that the person is absolved of the charge and prevents a retrial pursuant to the doctrine of double jeopardy.

Acquittal—One who is acquitted receives an acquittal, which is a release without further prosecution.

Adjourn—To briefly postpone or delay a court proceeding.

Adjudication—The determination of a controversy and pronouncement of judgment.

Admissible Evidence—Evidence which may be received by a trial court to assist the trier of fact, either the judge or jury, in deciding a dispute.

Admission—In criminal law, the voluntary acknowledgment that certain facts are true.

American Bar Association (ABA)—A national organization of lawyers and law students.

American Civil Liberties Union (ACLU)—A nationwide organization dedicated to the enforcement and preservation of rights and civil liberties guaranteed by the federal and state constitutions.

Amnesty—A pardon that excuses one of a criminal offense.

Appearance—To come into court, personally or through an attorney, after being summoned.

Arraign—In a criminal proceeding, to accuse one of committing a wrong.

Arraignment—The initial step in the criminal process when the defendant is formally charged with the wrongful conduct.

Arrest—To deprive a person of his liberty by legal authority.

Arson—The crime of intentionally setting fire to a building or other property.

Bail—Security, usually in the form of money, which is given to insure the future attendance of the defendant at all stages of a criminal proceeding.

Bail Bond—A document which secures the release of a person in custody, which is procured by security which is subject to forfeiture if the individual fails to appear.

Bailiff—An attendant of the court.

Battery—The unlawful application of force to the person of another.

Bench—The court and the judges composing the court collectively.

Bench Warrant—An order of the court empowering the police or other legal authority to seize a person.

Bias Incident—A crime caused by the criminal's animosity towards the victim's race, religion, ethnicity, or sexual orientation; a hate crime.

Bill of Rights—The first eight amendments to the United States Constitution.

Bodily Injury—Generally refers to any act, except one done in self-defense, that results in physical injury or sexual abuse.

Burden of Proof—The duty of a party to substantiate an allegation or issue to convince the trier of fact as to the truth of their claim.

Capacity—Capacity is the legal qualification concerning the ability of one to understand the nature and effects of one's acts.

Capital Crime—A crime for which the death penalty may, but need not necessarily, be imposed.

Capital Punishment—The penalty of death.

Child Abuse—Any form of cruelty to a child's physical, moral or mental well-being.

Child Custody—The care, control and maintenance of a child which may be awarded by a court to one of the parents of the child.

Child Protective Agency—A state agency responsible for the investigation of child abuse and neglect reports.

Child Support—The legal obligation of parents to contribute to the economic maintenance of their children.

Child Welfare—A generic term which embraces the totality of measures necessary for a child's well being; physical, moral and mental.

Circumstantial Evidence—Indirect evidence by which a principal fact may be inferred.

Concerted Action—An act which is planned and carried out between parties who are acting together.

Conclusive Evidence—Evidence which is incontrovertible.

Concurrent—In criminal law, refers to sentences which are to be served simultaneously.

Confession—In criminal law, an admission of guilt or other incriminating statement made by the accused.

Confidence Game—A scheme where the perpetrator wins the confidence of his or her victim in order to cheat the victim out of a sum of money or other valuable.

Confrontation Clause—A Sixth Amendment right of the Constitution which permits the accused in a criminal prosecution to confront the witness against him.

Consecutive—In criminal law, refers to sentences which are to be served in numerical order.

Consent Search—A search which is carried out with the voluntary authorization of the subject of the search.

Conspiracy—A scheme by two or more persons to commit a criminal or unlawful act.

Conspirator—One of the parties involved in a conspiracy.

Constitution—The fundamental principles of law which frame a governmental system.

Constitutional Right—Refers to the individual liberties granted by the constitution of a state or the federal government.

Court—The branch of government responsible for the resolution of disputes arising under the laws of the government.

Criminal Court—The court designed to hear prosecutions under the criminal laws.

Cross-Examination—The questioning of a witness by someone other than the one who called the witness to the stand concerning matters about which the witness testified during direct examination.

Cruel and Unusual Punishment—Refers to punishment that is shocking to the ordinary person, inherently unfair, or excessive in comparison to the crime committed.

Cruelty—The intentional and malicious infliction of physical or mental suffering on one's spouse.

District Attorney—An officer of a governmental body with the duty to prosecute those accused of crimes.

Docket—A list of cases on the court's calendar.

Domestic Violence—Generally refers to felony or misdemeanor crimes of violence committed by a current or former spouse of the victim, by a person with whom the victim shares a child in common, by a person who is cohabitating with or has cohabitated with the victim as a spouse, or by a person similarly situated to a spouse.

Double Jeopardy—Fifth Amendment provision providing that an individual shall not be subject to prosecution for the same offense more than one time.

Due Process Rights—All rights which are of such fundamental importance as to require compliance with due process standards of fairness and justice.

Entrapment—In criminal law, refers to the use of trickery by the police to induce the defendant to commit a crime for which he or she has a predisposition to commit.

Exclusionary Rule—A constitutional rule of law providing that evidence procured by illegal police conduct, although otherwise admissible, will be excluded at trial.

Eyewitness—A person who can testify about a matter because of his or her own presence at the time of the event.

Fact Finder—In a judicial or administrative proceeding, the person, or group of persons, that has the responsibility of determining the acts relevant to decide a controversy.

Fact Finding—A process by which parties present their evidence and make their arguments to a neutral person, who issues a nonbinding report based on the findings, which usually contains a recommendation for settlement.

Felony—A crime of a graver or more serious nature than those designated as misdemeanors.

Felony Murder—A first degree murder charge which results when a homicide occurs during the course of certain specified felonies, such as arson and robbery.

Fine—A financial penalty imposed upon a defendant.

Forfeiture—The loss of goods or chattels, as a punishment for some crime or misdemeanor of the party forfeiting, and as a compensation for the offense and injury committed against the one to whom they are forfeited.

Fraud—A false representation of a matter of fact, whether by words or by conduct, by false or misleading allegations, or by concealment of that which should have been disclosed.

Hearing—A proceeding to determine an issue of fact based on the evidence presented.

Hearsay Rule—The evidence rule that declares any statement, other than that by a witness who is testifying at the hearing, is not admissible as evidence to prove the truth of the matter asserted, unless it falls under an exception to the rule.

Homicide—The killing of a human being by another human being.

Hung Jury—A jury which cannot render a verdict because its members cannot reconcile their differences to a necessary standard, e.g. unanimity, substantial majority.

Illegal—Against the law.

Immunity—A benefit of exemption from a duty or penalty.

Impaneling—Selecting and swearing in a panel of jurors for duty.

Imprisonment—The confinement of an individual, usually as punishment for a crime.

Indictment—A formal written accusation of criminal charges submitted to a grand jury for investigation and indorsement.

Information—A written accusation of a crime submitted by the prosecutor to inform the accused and the court of the charges and the facts of the crime.

Injury—Any damage done to another's person, rights, reputation or property.

Jail—Place of confinement where a person in custody of the government awaits trial or serves a sentence after conviction.

Jailhouse Lawyer—An inmate who gains knowledge of the law through self-study, and assists fellow inmates in preparation of appeals, although he or she is not licensed to practice law.

Judge—The individual who presides over a court, and whose function it is to determine controversies.

Jury—A group of individuals summoned to decide the facts in issue in a lawsuit.

Jury Trial—A trial during which the evidence is presented to a jury so that they can determine the issues of fact, and render a verdict based upon the law as it applies to their findings of fact.

Larceny—The unlawful taking of the property of another, without his or her consent, with the intention of converting it to one's own use.

Law Enforcement—Generally refers to public agencies charged with policing functions, including any of their component bureaus.

Legal Aid—A national organization established to provide legal services to those who are unable to afford private representation.

Lineup—A police procedure whereby a suspect is placed in line with other persons of similar description so that a witness to the crime may attempt an identification.

Malice—A state of mind that accompanies the intentional commission of a wrongful act.

Manslaughter—The unlawful taking of another's life without malice aforethought.

Mens Rea—A guilty mind.

Misdemeanor—Criminal offenses which are less serious than felonies and carry lesser penalties.

Mistrial—A trial which is terminated prior to the return of a verdict, such as occurs when the jury is unable to reach a verdict.

Modus Operandi—Latin for "the manner of operation." Refers to the characteristic method used by a criminal in carrying out his or her actions.

National Domestic Violence Hotline—A national, toll-free telephone hotline operated for the purpose of providing information and assistance to victims of domestic violence.

Nolo Contendere—Latin for "I do not wish to contend." Statement by a defendant who does not wish to contest a charge. Although tantamount to a plea of guilty for the offense charged, it cannot be used against the defendant in another forum.

Not Guilty—The plea of a defendant in a criminal action denying the offense with which he or she is charged.

Obstruction of Justice—An offense by which one hinders the process by which individuals seek justice in the court, such as by intimidating jury members.

Offense—Any misdemeanor or felony violation of the law for which a penalty is prescribed.

Pardon—To release from further punishment, either conditionally or unconditionally.

Parole—The conditional release from imprisonment whereby the convicted individual serves the remainder of his or her sentence outside of prison as long as he or she is in compliance with the terms and conditions of parole.

Penal Institution—A place of confinement for convicted criminals.

Polygraph—A lie detector test.

Prejudice—A negative belief about a group of people who share a common characteristic, e.g. a particular race or religion.

Presumption of Innocence—In criminal law, refers to the doctrine that an individual is considered innocent of a crime until he or she is proven guilty.

Prisoner—One who is confined to a prison or other penal institution for the purpose of awaiting trial for a crime, or serving a sentence after conviction of a crime.

Probable Cause—The standard which must be met in order for there to be a valid search and seizure or arrest. It includes the showing of facts and circumstances reasonably sufficient and credible to permit the police to obtain a warrant.

Prosecution—The process of pursuing a civil lawsuit or a criminal trial.

Prosecutor—The individual who prepares a criminal case against an individual accused of a crime.

Protection Order—Generally refers to any injunction issued for the purpose of preventing violent or threatening acts of domestic violence or harassment, including temporary and final orders issued by civil or criminal courts.

Public Defender—A lawyer hired by the government to represent an indigent person accused of a crime.

Racial Slur—A negative remark that demonstrates a racial prejudice.

Restitution—The act of making an aggrieved party whole by compensating him or her for any loss or damage sustained.

Robbery—The felonious act of stealing from a person, by the use of force or the threat of force, so as to put the victim in fear.

Search and Seizure—The search by law enforcement officials of a person or place in order to seize evidence to be used in the investigation and prosecution of a crime.

Search Warrant—A judicial order authorizing and directing law enforcement officials to search a specified location for specific items or individuals.

Self-Defense—The right to protect oneself, one's family, and one's property from an aggressor.

Sentence—The punishment given a convicted criminal by the court.

Subpoena—A court issued document compelling the appearance of a witness before the court.

Summons—A mandate requiring the appearance of the defendant in an action under penalty of having judgment entered against him for failure to do so.

Suppression of Evidence—The refusal to produce or permit evidence for use in litigation, such as when there has been an illegal search and seizure of the evidence.

Suspended Sentence—A sentence which is not executed contingent upon the defendant's observance of certain court-order terms and conditions.

Taking the Fifth—The term given to an individual's right not to incriminate oneself under the Fifth Amendment.

Testify—The offering of a statement in a judicial proceeding, under oath and subject to the penalty of perjury.

Testimony—The sworn statement make by a witness in a judicial proceeding.

Transferred Intent—The doctrine which provides that if a defendant intends harm to A, but harms B instead, the intent is deemed transferred to B, as far as the defendant's liability to B in tort is concerned.

Unreasonable Search and Seizure—A search and seizure which has not met the constitutional requirements under the Fourth and Fourteenth Amendment.

Verdict—The definitive answer given by the jury to the court concerning the matters of fact committed to the jury for their deliberation and determination.

Victim Services—Generally refers to organizations that assist domestic violence or sexual assault victims, such as rape crisis centers and battered women's shelters.

Warrant—An official order directing that a certain act be undertaken, such as an arrest.

Warrantless Arrest—An arrest carried out without a warrant.

White Collar Crime—Refers to a class of nonviolent offenses which have their basis in fraud and dishonesty.

Wrongful Death Statute—A statute that creates a cause of action for any wrongful act, neglect, or default that causes death.

BIBLIOGRAPHY AND ADDITIONAL READING

Black's Law Dictionary, Fifth Edition. St. Paul, MN: West Publishing Company, 1979.

Communities Against Violence Network (CAVNET) (Date Visited: November 2003) <http://www.cavnet.org>.

The Centers for Disease Control and Prevention: National Institute for Occupational Safety and Health (Date Visited: November 2003) <http://www.cdc.gov/niosh/homepage.html>.

The Domestic Violence Hotline Resource List (Date Visited: November 2003) <http://www.feminist.org/911/crisis.html>.

The Elder Abuse Prevention Information & Resource Guide (Date Visited: November 2003) <http://www.oaktrees.org/elder/>.

Evaluation Guidebook: Projects Funded by S.T.O.P. Formula Grants under the Violence Against Women Act (Date Visited: November 2003) <http://www.urban.org/crime/evalguide.html>.

Justice Information Center (Date Visited: November 2003) <http://www.ncjrs.org/>

The National Coalition Against Sexual Assault (Date Visited: November 2003) <http://www.achiever.com/freehmpg/ncas/>.

The National Domestic Violence Hotline (Date Visited: November 2003) <http://www.ndvh.org/>.

Office of Justice Programs (Date Visited: November 2003) <http://www.ojp.usdog.gov/>.

Rape, Abuse and Incest National Network (Date Visited: November 2003) <http://www.rainn.org/>.

The U.S. Department of Health and Human Services (Date Visited: November 2003) <http://www.os.dhhs.gov/>.

The U.S. Department of Justice (Date Visited: November 2003) <http://www.usdoj.gov/>.